Best Practices
Interdisciplinary Vocabulary Development
The Rule of 3

Linda D. Ventriglia, Ph.D.

The Teaching Collection includes the following titles:

Best Practices Interdisciplinary Vocabulary Development
The Rule of 3

Best Practices Differentiated Instruction
The Rule of Foot

Best Practices Motivation and Student Engagement
Creating Power Learners

Best Practices Interdisciplinary Literacy
Stoplight Strategies

Best Practices for English Language Learning
A Conversational Approach to Language and Literacy

Best Practices 21st Century Questioning and Problem Solving
Infolinking

Best Practices for 21st Century Teaching
The EduRevolution

Cover Design: Jesus Salcedo

8th edition
© 2009 by Linda D. Ventriglia, Ph.D.
ISBN 978-1-931277-01-3
Printed in Mexico

This book was printed in June 2009 at
Litográfica Ingramex, S.A. de C.V. Centeno 162-1,
Col. Granjas Esmeralda C.P. 09810, México, D.F.

Younglight
E D U C A T E
Light Up the Mind

The Younglight logo—a bright sun—represents lighting up the mind through learning. Younglight is committed to accelerating the achievement of all learners through professional development books that give teachers a repertoire of research-based Best Practices in teaching. By providing teachers with a repertoire of instructional strategies, Younglight carries out the promise of its logo, books that *Light Up the Mind.*

Visit www.younglighteducate.com
to find more educational titles in the
Best Practices series of books.

Preface to the Best Practices in Classroom Instruction Series

Quality Teaching: The Best Predictor of High Student Achievement

Student achievement is based on quality teaching. High quality teaching, along with stimulating interaction between students and teachers, ensures all students' academic success. This *Best Practices* classroom instruction series is based on the belief that teachers are the greatest resource available to students today.

Proven research-based *Best Practices* in this series provide teachers with a full repertoire of the instructional strategies needed to create optimal learning opportunities for diverse learners. These instructional strategies increase student achievement by focusing instruction on the content standards which are aligned with state assessments.

The Best Practice books and accompanying CD's are the result of ten years of school-based research. Schools that implemented the strategies outlined in the Best Practices in Classroom Instruction Series showed significantly greater gains in achievement than schools which were matched for: socioeconomic status, percentage of free and reduced lunch, transience, attendance, student population and percentage of English learners. School wide adherence to Best Practices teaching—including differentiated instruction based on standards-based eight week benchmarks—resulted in dramatic gains in students' achievement. Academic improvement was palpable starting when the strategies were first employed, and gains continued year after year. Schools have achieved gold and distinguished status. Some teachers have become National Board certified.

Teachers using Best Practices reported that their

classrooms were forever positively changed. Students became more engaged in learning. Best Practice teaching strategies challenged students to push the limits of their thinking to higher levels of problem solving. This changed the dynamics of learning in the classroom. Students became more thoughtful about what they were learning. They became more self motivated. As Team Leaders in cooperative groups, students mentored each other. The teacher's role changed from a director of learning to a facilitator of learning.

Best Practice teachers noted that after three years, the teaching strategies and classroom groupings became an integral part of how content was delivered and learned in their classrooms. Teachers at Best Practice schools established a learning community that went beyond their schools. The Best Practice concept of "teachers helping teachers" was implemented as teachers served as coaches and mentors of other teachers. This had a significant impact on teacher empowerment. It was the expertise of teachers reflecting on, modeling and implementing Best Practices that ultimately created success for all students.

Interdiscipinary Vocabulary Development is the first book in the Best Practices series. It is first because research shows there is nothing that correlates more with school success than vocabulary. There is a 99.9% correlation between a student's vocabulary and school achievement. Research shows that 20 minutes of structured vocabulary instruction a day results in accelerated achievement for students across content areas. This book outlines the powerful *Rule of 3* as a systematic approach for accelerated vocabulary development.

Table of Contents

* Best Practices in Vocabulary Development dvd accompanies this manual.

Best Practices in Vocabulary Development

Chapter 1

Interdisciplinary Vocabulary Development: Lingolinking

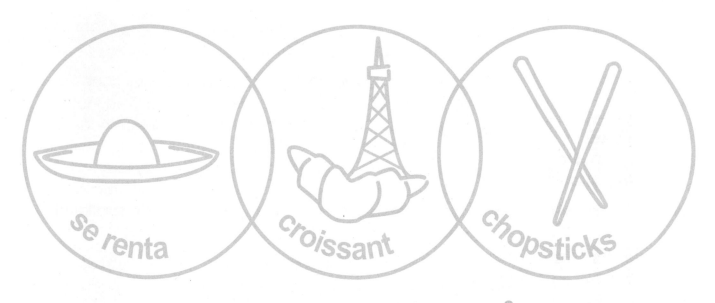

In the past, vocabulary instruction was assumed to be the job of the elementary school reading teacher or the middle school or high school language arts teacher. The educational research on Best Practices indicates that students' school success in the 21st Century depends on all teachers across disciplines becoming skilled in helping students acquire academic vocabulary.

Recent research further demonstrates that interdisciplinary vocabulary development helps close the achievement gap for struggling students and English language learners.

Interdisciplinary Instruction

What is interdisciplinary teaching? The term interdisciplinary is defined as studies that cut across several established disciplines or fields of study. Interdisciplinary teaching connects and integrates several academic disciplines along with their specific perspectives.

It includes instructing students in the process of how to find and integrate information across disciplines to address a particular theme or to solve a problem. Interdisciplinary instruction encourages students to analyze and evaluate information from multiple viewpoints (Klein, 2008).

The basis of interdisciplinary instruction has historical antecedents with Greek philosophers. They believed that: knowledge of any subject can be best understood by combining and synthesizing ideas from various disciplines. Thus, the goal of interdisciplinary learning was to transcend disciplines to discover insights into established thinking or to come up with new solutions for old problems.

The basis of interdisciplinary instruction has historical antecedents with Greek philosophers. They believed that: knowledge of any subject can be best understood by combining and synthesizing ideas from various disciplines.

This Greek philosophy of having students form concepts across disciplines made sense in theory. Yet, schools were not sure how to transfer this theory into practice. The educational bureaucracy in the 20th century was wedded to the idea that subjects could be learned more easily by keeping them as separate disciplines. Each subject was considered an entity of knowledge. The vocabulary and concepts attached to that subject were considered for the most part, exclusive to that particular discipline.

The compartmentalization of subject areas seemed to be justifiable in an era where education was based on the industrial model. Consider how the traditional industrial model operated. Each activity was separated. The worker completed only one part of the process. He or she was not required to understand the whole manufacturing process. Information was limited and segregated.

The model of subject-directed education that seemed to fit the 20th century mind set both in theory and in practice is rapidly becoming outdated in the 21st century. Information is no longer limited and easily segregated into subject disciplines.

Technology has made factual knowledge seemingly limitless. The proliferation of hundreds of thousands of facts has made it necessary for workers in every profession to synthesize and integrate information. Knowledge is no longer linear. It is nonlinear.

Think about how information is accessed on the computer. You may be reading along and then click on a link and be off in a new direction of learning. As each of the links is explored, the information must be synthesized and integrated. And so we have come full circle back to the Greek philosophers. The learners' task is to integrate information and form concepts across disciplines.

The difference now is that students have powerful technology to facilitate the process. Yet even with technology, the process of interdisciplinary information synthesizing is not easy for many students. It requires creativity and thinking. It also demands that learners have the global academic vocabulary to find information and crosslink facts across subject areas.

Many students do not have the word knowledge base to function successfully in the 21st century Conceptual Age which requires students to read more, more and more words and integrate more, more and more facts (Pink, 2006). They have not developed the academic vocabulary needed to read and comprehend information using digital or text-based content resources.

Academic Vocabulary Development and Subject-Area Frameworks

Have you ever been to a low achieving school and visited the library? Did you find the adopted science or history textbooks on the shelves in the book closet? What did the librarian respond when you asked why the books were not being used? Did he or she say that the students cannot read them?

The question now that you must ask yourself is why the students can't read the books. It is most likely because they do not have the vocabulary to comprehend the text. So the vicious circle starts; students need the information to master a subject discipline but they can't read the text. This scenario is especially true for English language learners and struggling readers.

> *The proliferation of hundreds of thousands of facts has made it necessary for every profession to crosslink and synthesize learning. Knowledge is no longer linear. Technology has made knowledge nonlinear.*

Students' inability to comprehend academic vocabulary acervates their low achievement and increases the achievement gap.

Students knowledge of words is just as important in science, mathematics and social studies as it is in English language arts.

Consider this United States history example that reflects the vocabulary load given to eighth graders:

> *Sectionalism caused a definite problem in 1828 when Congress imposed a high tariff on imports. The tariff was supposed to help the northern factory owners sell their manufactured goods because it increased the cost of European goods* (adapted from *Early United States*, 2002).

This short excerpt of two sentences contains at least ten words that may be new or difficult for struggling readers and English learners. These words are *sectionalism, caused, definite, imposed, tariff, imports, manufactured, increased, European,* and *goods.* Students need to have a well developed word knowledge base to handle the demands of this excerpt (Harmon et al., 2005).

Even if students can decode the words in the excerpt, they still may not comprehend what the vocabulary words mean. The definition of reading vocabulary is the number of words that are decoded and *understood.* Decoding the word *sectionalism* does nothing for students who have not learned the meaning of this subject-specific vocabulary word. They must also understand the interdisciplinary words *caused, definite, manufactured* and *increased.* Students need a formidable academic vocabulary to understand what they are reading.

Research has clearly shown that students' reading comprehension across disciplines is heavily dependent on their knowledge of academic vocabulary. The term *academic vocabulary* refers to word knowledge that makes it possible for students to engage with, produce and talk about texts that are valued in schools (Brozo and Simpson, 2007).

> **Research has clearly shown that students' reading comprehension across disciplines is heavily dependent on their knowledge of academic vocabulary.**

The relationship of academic vocabulary to overall subject-area reading comprehension was confirmed through a Rand Reading Study Group Report. The data showed that there was a highly significant relationship between vocabulary knowledge and overall reading comprehension. Furthermore, the study revealed that this relationship is even more significant for content texts due to the burden they place on students to understand new and numerous technical subject-related words (Harmon, Hedrick and Wood, 2005). Students need to possess the academic vocabulary necessary to explore information and concepts in content area materials.

State subject area frameworks validate the importance of academic vocabulary as integral to the study of each discipline. Each subject area framework contains a "glossary" of words that are crucial to the study of the discipline. Some of the words that are included in the glossary for the mathematics framework include *algorithm, asymptote, axiom, binomial, congruent, conjecture, corollary, dilation, exponent, function, hypothesis, inequality, integers, mean, parallel, postulate, quartiles symmetry* and *variable*.

In addition to having a glossary of words, all subject-area state frameworks affirm the importance of the teacher explicitly teaching academic vocabulary to their students.

In addition to having a glossary of words, all the subject area state frameworks affirm the importance of the teacher explicitly teaching academic vocabulary to their students. The California state framework for science states:

> *Effective science programs develop students' command of the academic language of science used in the content standards. Studying science involves acquiring new vocabulary and learning that "interdisciplinary" words may have different meanings in science. The scientific vocabulary that is important for building conceptual understanding in science must be taught explicitly. Teachers need to provide clear explanations of new terms and idioms by using words and examples that are clear and precise. New subject-specific words like "photosynthesis" must be taught along with the definitions of interdisciplinary words like " table" that need to be expanded to incorporate specific meanings in science* (Science Framework for the California Public Schools, 2004).

The Science Framework addresses both the subject specific words and the *interdisciplinary words* that must be taught and understood in the context of science. For example, the terms *control* and *theory* have different definitions in science than other subject disciplines. Just as the terms *net* and *order* have different definitions in mathamatics than in other subject disciplines.

Scientific terms may have Greek and Latin roots such as biology (Greek) and animal (Latin). Students need to know Latin and Greek roots to comprehend the meaning of words in science textbooks and supplementary materials.

The science framework confirms the importance of Latin roots, Greek roots, prefixes and suffixes for students' comprehension of academic vocabulary in science.

The framework notes: *An understanding of root words and affixes will not only improve vocabulary but increase students' ability to comprehend words they have not encountered before.* For example, it helps students to know that biology is a combination of *bio-* (derived from the Greek word for *life*) and *-logy* (also rooted in Greek) that means *study* (Science Framework for the California Public Schools, 2004). Thus, the framework emphasizes the need for teaching both subject-specific words and interdisciplinary words.

State subject area frameworks across the United States address the critical need to instruct all students, including English learners, in academic vocabulary. The need is thought to be critical because as the demand of advanced literacy skills in content areas increases, the ability to read and comprehend an expanded number of interdisciplinary words becomes very important.

> **State subject area frameworks across the United States address the critical need to instruct all students, including English learners, in academic vocabulary.**

Interdisciplinary Vocabulary Development

Finding the time for direct instruction of large numbers of words from the content areas presents teachers with a major challenge (Anderson and Nagy, 1991). Building students' vocabulary across disciplines to be truly effective requires the teacher to be highly selective in choosing the words that are targeted for instruction.

Academic vocabulary can be easily taught when words are placed in three tiers. *Tier one words* include basic sight words and *cognates*, which are words that look similar and mean the same thing in two languages. Spanish and English, for example, have many cognates, such as *family* and *familia*, *triangle* and *triángulo*, and *metaphor* and *metáfora*.

Tier two words are critical interdisciplinary words, such as *hypothesize, interrelate, decipher.* These words are used across subject areas. Multiple meaning words are grouped with tier two words. Words like *table* are multiple meaning words. This word has a specific subject area interpretation, a table of numbers in math or science, as well as other meanings.

Tier three words include vocabulary that is limited to specific subject domains. All subject areas have tier three words. These words are learned by students in subject context. Tier three words also include idioms, such as *underground railroad* in social studies, *guinea pig* in science and *square a number* in mathematics (Calderon, 2004).

The subject frameworks refer to two types of academic vocabulary words that must be taught to students. These are the subject specific words and the academic vocabulary that cross disciplines. This can be interpreted to mean that the teacher needs to focus on tier two and tier three words for academic vocabulary development. This does not mean that students do not need to learn tier one sight words. They do. But once students have mastered these words, then the focus for content text comprehension clearly needs to be on tier two and tier three words.

Academic vocabulary can be most easily taught when words are placed in three tiers.

Tier one words include basic sight words and cognates.

Tier two words are critical interdisciplinary words that cross subject areas and words that have multiple meanings.

Tier three words are vocabulary and idioms limited to a specific subject.

Consider the words that are contained in just one science standard for fifth-grade physical science: *Students know scientists have developed instruments that can create discrete images of atoms and molecules that show that atoms and molecules can occur in well-ordered arrays.* The tier three subject specific words are: *atoms, molecules, scientists.* Interdisciplinary tier two words in this standard include: *developed, instruments, create, discrete, images, well-ordered,* and *arrays.*

It is hypothesized, based on numerous vocabulary development studies, that if content teachers focused on teaching interdisciplinary words as well as their subject-specific words, this would result in students' increased comprehension of content texts. It would also help to close the achievement gap for struggling readers and English learners (Kamil, 2004).

There are approximately 1200 interdisciplinary words per grade level that have been identified as critical for students to comprehend core subject-area texts and trade books (younglighteducate.com). These words are learned most effectively when they are tied to words that are limited to specific domains such as science, social studies, health or math. For example, the word *system* is a critical fifth-grade tier two, multiple meaning word. The meaning of this word is best taught to students across subject disciplines. The teacher can highlight the meaning of the word in a discussion on the United States *system* of government. It can be reinforced in math to explain a *system* for calculating percentages, in science to label a *system* of the body, or in physical education to describe a series of plays. Providing multiple exposures to critical words is cited by research as one of the most effective ways to expand word learning in the content areas and consequently increase student achievement (Pearson, et al. 2007).

While it may seem on the surface that it is much easier for the elementary teacher to reinforce a critical word across disciplines, this is not necessarily true. Middle school and high school subject area teachers who collaborate can be just as effective in teaching critical interdisciplinary words.

> *Providing multiple exposures to critical words is cited by research as one of the most effective ways to expand word learning in the content areas and consequently increase student achievement.*

Think about how the critical multiple meaning word *cell* can be taught using a interdisciplinary approach. The high school biology teacher can teach students the meaning of a *cell* in the body. The history teacher can engage students in a discussion on the *cell* phone and its impact on communication. The word *cell* may be highlighted by the language arts teacher to refer to a person incarcerated in a *cell*.

An interdisciplinary approach for a science unit on stem *cell* research in the treatment of diabetes can develop other tenth grade critical tier two words around the concept. These words include: *repress, graph, proliferate, propelled, derived, propensity, intractable, health, precautions, research* and *experimental*.

Learning these tier two words is easier for students when the vocabulary is connected through interdisciplinary teaching units. The science standard: *The fundamental processes of plants and animals depend on a variety of chemical reactions that occur in specialized areas of the organism's cells* can be used as the basis for targeting key vocabulary related to stem cell research. After students study stem cell research from a scientific perspective, an interdisciplinary social studies connection could involve two teams of students in a debate on whether to allow research with embryonic cell cultures in the United States (Wade, 2008). Students thus learn to apply the tier 2 words *derived, propensity* and *intractable* across the disciplines of science and social studies.

Mathematics is integrated in the unit as students find statistics to support their position on stem cell research. Students use the targeted tier two words *research, graph* and *derived* as they create charts, graphs and tables to display the data from research. Students incorporate information from global health literature to document case histories of people who have benefited or failed to benefit from the stem cell research.

This interdisciplinary science unit teaches both subject matter information and critical tier two vocabulary words. Students can be instructed by a science teacher in this interdisciplinary unit or by a team of teachers who work together to expose students to tier two critical words in different subject contexts.

Tying Tier Two Words to Subject Concepts

Consider a fifth grade lesson on the geography of the United States that addresses the social studies standard: *Students know the location of the current 50 states and the names of their capitals.* The tier three subject-specific words students must learn are *United States, North America* and *country.* Fifth grade critical interdisciplinary words tied to the learning of the content standard include: *edge, border, connect, exterior, adjacent, diagonal, side, boundary, borders, direction* and *position.* These words can be thought of as a critical cluster of tier two vocabulary related to United States' geography. A map of the United States and targeted questioning can help students master the meaning of these words.

What states are adjacent to Arizona?

In what direction would you drive to get to California from Utah?

What country borders the state of Washington?

The goal is for the teacher to immerse students in learning academic vocabulary as they master a content standard. While it is important that students learn specific subject-related words, it is the tier two interdisciplinary words that accelerate the building of word power. Teaching standards-based academic terminology enhances students' ability to read and understand subject-area content. It ultimately helps students build a store of academic word knowledge that accelerates academic achievement (Marzano, 2005).

Clustering Interdisciplinary Words

Interdisciplinary tier two words can also be learned through a clustering approach using graphic organizers. This approach groups words around a subject concept, such as *government institutions*. Math terms can be clustered around types of equations. Language arts words can be connected and grouped as object concepts, event concepts, action concepts and movement concepts (Marzano,1998). Words can be tied by associations and presented in a graphic organizer. Below is an example of a cluster of terms grouped around the concept of measurement actions.

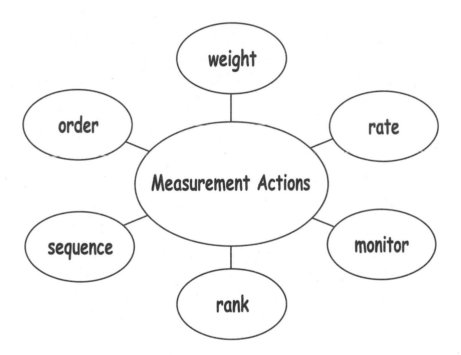

You may notice that all these words are tier two words. The words can be applied to other subject areas in addition to mathematics. Beck, McKeown and Omanson (2002) state that the selection of words to be taught must be dependent and independent of the classroom curriculum. Teachers must select those words that have the most transferability to other subjects, to news events and to students' daily lives.

According to researchers, teachers need to select academic vocabulary applicable to other subject disciplines. The concept of cross-linking goes beyond language arts, math, history and science. A broader net needs to be cast to

examine vocabulary instruction throughout the school day (Scott et al., 2003). This means that interdisciplinary words should extend to health, physical education, music, art, and other school subjects.

Students can learn words with multiple meanings, such as *play, center* and *guard* as applied to the sport of basketball. These words can also be learned across disciplines. The word *play* can also be applied to music, *center* to social studies and *guard* to language arts. Exposure to words does not have to be limited to the school environment. Students can utilize learned vocabulary in their social and academic conversations.

Repeated exposures to words are valuable. Each exposure adds information on how the words are used in context and how they are connected to other disciplines. (Blachowitz and Fisher, 2000). It is through the multiple exposures to words, including semantic relations among words, that students build a rich understanding of word meaning.

The fact is that students need to learn and become conversant with the 88,500 words that have been estimated by researchers to be critical to the understanding of subject matter books in grades three through nine

The fact is that students need to learn and become conversant with the 88,500 words that have been estimated by researchers to be critical to the understanding of subject matter books in grades three through nine (Nagy, 1997). Interdisciplinary vocabulary development gives students some practice with the 171,476 English words written in the Oxford dictionary and with at least a significant number of the 988,968 words that are part of an Internet global vocabulary. If these numbers seem staggering, consider once again that exposure, just becoming aware of the meaning of words, is a significant factor in vocabulary development.

Interdisciplinary Vocabulary Development Strategies

The goal of all vocabulary instruction is for students to get meaning from the written word. This meaning must be both academic and personal. Strategies that build meaning include relating words to students' background knowledge and inferring the meaning of words from context.

Other strategies include: recording academic and personal meaning of words in a notebook, identifying Greek and Latin roots and learning how to interpret words according to an author's meaning. These general meaning-based strategies have been noted by researchers to be critical for students' understanding of increasingly challenging texts across subject areas (Nelson, 2000).

Meaning-based strategies that help students master interdisciplinary vocabulary must be learned through textual applications as well as digital applications. There are a number of online resources that help students master vocabulary words. These resources include dictionary.com, thesaurus.com, synonym.com and antonym.com. Students need to learn to use these quick references to develop a rich written and oral vocabulary across subject areas.

Interdisciplinary Writing and Vocabulary Development

Many researchers have identified a rich vocabulary as the single most important factor in reading comprehension (LaFlamme, 1997). There is, likewise, a myriad of studies that link vocabulary development to the ability to write well across disciplines. The ability to write effectively has been noted by linguists to be more closely related to vocabulary than even reading. During the reading process, students can often infer the meaning of words from the context. However when students write, they must think of the words to put on paper or type on the computer. The words must come, so to speak, out of their heads. Writing is especially difficult for English learners who do not have the breath and depth of the English vocabulary needed for effective written communication. It is writing, not the oral communication or reading, that is the stumbling block for the redesignation of many English learners.

Oftentimes, writing is thought to be the responsibility of the language arts teacher. Yet, an interdisciplinary approach to writing has been shown to be most effective.

The ability to write effectively has been noted by linguists to be more closely related to vocabulary than even reading.

Research confirms that written communication is more effective when the depth of vocabulary and command of language is evident (Venet, 2008).

Interdisciplinary words are learned most effectively when they are tied to a culminating writing activity. If students can create a meaningful written discourse, the teacher can feel assured that they have mastered a significant number of vocabulary words.

If students can explain a math principle in writing, the teacher can be assured that students have learned critical math vocabulary words. Students who can compose an argument to support one of two points of view on a historical event, have a good grasp of words relating to history or social science. Students who can write up a science experiment and explain their conclusions have indeed mastered key scientific terms. Written discourse is one of the best ways for the teacher to assess not only what students have learned in a unit, but also how they can use subject-specific and interdisciplinary vocabulary. It is the interdisciplinary vocabulary used effectively in communication that prepares students to be successful in the 21st century global linguistic community.

It is the interdisciplinary vocabulary used effectively in communication that prepares students to be successful in the 21st century global linguistic community.

Lingolinking

The active learning of vocabulary enables students to make connections, communicate and access information on the Internet. These cognitive connections include the schematic knowledge needed to create digital forms of communication. Students need a broad mastery of vocabulary to become part of the larger 21st century global linguistic community.

The Internet and other instant communication tools have enabled words to be easily transferred from one language to another. Words from around the world are increasingly becoming integrated into English. The integration of words from one global language to another is termed *lingolinking* (Ventriglia, 2008).

During recent years many Spanish language words have been integrated into the English language.

You can now find the word *tortillas* in most standard English dictionaries in the United States. While the word remains part of the Spanish language, the word has through usage become part of the English language. The Spanish word has been linked to the English language as both English speakers and Spanish speakers use the same word to describe a round flat food made of corn or wheat flour masa. This is an example of lingolinking.

Another global word that has become linked to English is the French word croissant. This crescent shaped roll has become linked to other concept words for bakery items that were traditionally part of the English language such as, bread and muffins. There are also linked words that have their origin in China. Chopsticks is a word used by Chinese as well as English speakers. Likewise the Chinese word tofu has largely replaced its English meaning bean curd. The word tofu has been linked to the English language and has become associated with vegetarian cuisine. The whole idea of lingolinking is the need to communicate in the most economical way possible. For example, it is easier to use the word sushi to relay the idea of individually portioned balls of rice topped with vegetables or raw fish.

It is not only the people in the United States that are busily adopting and integrating a set of global words into the English language; people from other countries are adding global words to their languages as well.

If you visit Mexico City and look around neighborhoods, you will see signs displayed on houses and apartments that read *Se Renta*. This sign is clear to every Spanish speaker who needs an accommodation. Actually, the verb *rentar* has the same meaning as the English words "to rent." The word *rentar* has through usage largely replaced the traditional Spanish word *alquilar,* which means "to rent" or "to lease." The German word "hamburger" has been adopted globally to refer to a meat patty between a bread bun. Recent trends in the global words include technological terms like microprocessor and cyberspace.

As we become more and more a part of an integrated global society, lingolinking or the linking of words from global communities, will become increasingly common. As words from across continents become linked, our cultures also become linked.

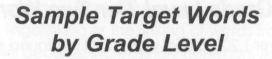

Sample Target Words
by Grade Level

Ninth Grade Target Words: accentuate, adept, callous, ardor, complement, crucial, daily, dilemma, enthrall, eradicate, evaluate, equilibrium, ethical

Tenth Grade Target Words: conveyance, courier, delve, emboss, eloquent, disreputable, exploit, futile, genteel, glutton, impoverish, inaccessible, incite, incandescent, inclination, invoke, materialize, maul, misconception, narrate, necessitate, negotiate parochial, passive, pinnacle, portal

Eleventh Grade Target Words: abashed, abdicate, annals, askew, arbitration, broach, carouse, cite, centrifugal, commentary, concave. compatible, convex, cosmopolitan, devious, dexterity, egotism, engross enliven, ensue, fraudulent, fervor, generalize, forage, immaterial, imperil, infamous, infest, inane

Twelfth Grade Target Words: incredulous, immobile, fastidious, inept, infest, infidelity, influx, inherent, intercede, instigate, literal, lobbyist, manifold, libel lunar, malign, malice, mandatory, manifest, manifold, mannerism, marauder, materialistic, meander, memento

Think About Discussion Questions

1. Evaluate at least 20 glossary words in the framework of the subject area you teach or in one of your core subject adopted textbooks. List and classify the glossary words as either tier 3 subject specific words or tier 2 interdisciplinary words. If you are an elementary teacher categorize at least 20 words from the math framework.

   The California standards and frameworks can be found at the California Department of Education website.

   If you teach in another state, go to your state's standards and frameworks website or use your adopted subject texts.

2. Think about the list of glossary words. Reflect on how you would integrate at least ten of these words to teach a content standard. Include at least five tier 2 words.

Reflection on Interdisciplinary Vocabulary Development

1. Reflect on a subject area standard that you teach. Create a graphic organizer with a cluster of interdisciplinary words that relate to the standard or a concept that the standard addresses.

2. Reflect on the writing process as it applies to the subject you teach or one of the subjects you teach, excluding language arts. Review the writing standards for your grade level. Describe how you would create an interdisciplinary activity that would apply the writing standards to your content area or one of the content areas you teach other than language arts.

Chapter 2
From Theory to Practice

The Theory

As teachers face increasingly diverse students who need to learn the language of success in schooling, the need to align interdisciplinary vocabulary instruction with research-based knowledge of vocabulary acquisition is critical and essential.

The Practice

Even though teachers play a unique role in vocabulary development for students, the amount of time spent on word learning in the classroom is severely limited. An analysis of vocabulary instruction revealed that only 6% of classroom time was devoted to developing vocabulary in language arts and 1.4% of time was spent on developing word knowledge in the other core subject areas (Scott, et al. 2003).

Building Vocabulary from Theory to Practice

Is there empirical evidence to confirm the theory that vocabulary development is critical for students' success in school? How does this theory translate into classroom practice?

Research confirms the hypothesis that time spent on a rich environment for vocabulary development does matter. Even the powerful correlations between low social economics and success in school are mitigated by extensive word knowledge. Weizman and Snow, (2004) found a powerful link between sophisticated word use of low income mothers and their children's success in school. Mothers who had an extensive vocabulary and supported the expanded vocabulary in the home had children who performed at higher academic levels. Other researchers have noted that the vocabulary subtest on I.Q. verbal measures has the highest correlation with overall I.Q.

For students learning to read, much of the meaning of written words is based directly on their oral understanding. If the meaning of words is understood, then it is much easier to attach written labels. If students have no background knowledge that ties meaning to the words, then learning to read the words is much more difficult. This can be noted in the following sentence: *Vamos a cenar en un restaurante.*

If you do not understand Spanish, the words have no meaning. Even if you deciphered the word restaurant, the message in the rest of the sentence is meaningless. If you have no oral understanding of the language, reading in the language fails to fulfill its main goal, "to get meaning from the written word."

> **Research confirms the hypothesis that time spent on a rich environment for vocabulary development does matter. Even the powerful correlations between low social economics and success in school are mitigated by extensive word knowledge.**

Word Knowledge and Literacy Acquisition

There is a correlation between oral language proficiency and the acquisition of literacy. The average middle-class English-speaking first grader has a vocabulary of about 10,000 words; the average third grader has between 14,000 and 24,000 words. The average growth in vocabulary from grades 3 to 12 is about 4,000 words a year (Graves, Slater and White 2002). Research studies have found a difference of about 5,300 words between 8 year olds of upper versus lower socioeconomic status. Middle class first grade students were shown to read and understand about 50% more words than economically disadvantaged first grade students (Graves, 2002). English language learners enter first grade with a vocabulary ranging from 10 to 2,000 words in English.

Why is the number of words which students know the meaning of significant? Research suggests that once decoding skills are mastered, insufficient knowledge of word meanings is the chief remaining barrier to school success for economically disadvantaged and English learners. Knowledge of word meaning facilitates the climb up the ladder to academic success. The following chart depicts SAT 9 National Achievement test results of a second grade class of English learners. These students have learned word study skills, structural analysis and vowel analysis.

The teacher has moved English learners in this class from the 20th to the 40th percentile in reading in one year. It can be noted, however, that the weakest subtests are reading vocabulary and multiple word meanings.

> *Research suggests that once decoding skills are mastered, insufficient knowledge of word meanings is the chief remaining barrier to school success for economically disadvantaged students and English learners.*

English Learners' Scores on SAT 9	Percentile
Word Study Skills	58
Structural Analysis	52
Vowel Analysis	50
Reading Vocabulary	25
Reading Comprehension	32
Multiple Word Meaning	23

Becker's study in the *Harvard Educational Review* stated that limited vocabulary knowledge was the principal factor in the school failure of economically disadvantaged students. He proposed systematic instruction of basic vocabulary of about 5,000 words as a solution. Graves, confirming Becker's research, further noted that schools fail to teach vocabulary systematically and that a basic vocabulary of 7,000 words a year should be taught beginning in first grade (Graves, et al., 2002).

The failure of schools to teach vocabulary is related to the limited amount of direct instruction prescribed in teachers' guides of basal reading series. Jaeger-Adams, (1996) and Walsh (2003) found that none of the most widely used basal content readers provided the attention to the vocabulary necessary to increase comprehension. Watts (1995) observed reading lessons in their entirety and found that vocabulary instruction occurred only in 10% of the observations. Durkin observed that of the 4,469 minutes of reading instruction, only 19 minutes were directed toward vocabulary instruction. Juel observed that third, fourth, and fifth grade teachers spent an average of 1.67 minutes on vocabulary per reading lesson. Besides the limited time spent on vocabulary instruction, the researchers noted that the words listed for instruction in reading basals were already familiar to most students. Methodical instruction of unknown vocabulary words was found to be absent from most classrooms (Juel, 1983).

> **Becker's study in the Harvard Educational Review stated that limited vocabulary knowledge was the principal factor in the school failure of disadvantaged students.**

Classroom Practice and Vocabulary Instruction in the Content Areas

Language arts is a core content area where the focus of teaching from kindergarten through high school is on literacy and writing skills. Research has confirmed that the development of vocabulary is integral to literacy skills. Yet, Blanton and Moorman (1990) noted that vocabulary was the focus of instruction in only 6% of the time spent in language arts instruction. They discovered that few teachers spent the time needed to create more than a superficial understanding of words central to the concepts they were trying to convey. Teachers did mention and assign words but provided very scant systematic instruction.

The limited amount of classroom time targeted to teaching word meaning is related directly to the minimal emphasis given vocabulary in subject area texts. Research studies have confirmed that there is less than 5% of instructional time devoted to the development of vocabulary in core subject texts other than language arts. Even in the most effective language arts series, only about 300 words are emphasized.

Furthermore, language arts textbooks include instructional recommendations that encourage the use of definition and context clues with no emphasis on generative word meaning. Jenkins and Dixon note that language arts texts do not rely much on direct teaching to develop students' vocabulary. Rather, they seem to take the position either that vocabulary is not an important part of schooling or that it occurs through incidental learning (Walsh, 2003).

The problem is even more acute in academic disciplines outside of language arts. Durkin examined the vocabulary development in social studies lessons. She found that only 3% of total instruction was focused on activities to enhance word meanings. Vocabulary words that were central to the understanding of social studies concepts were not emphasized. There was even less time devoted to the development of interdisciplinary vocabulary words that were critical for the understanding of the core text's presentation of information relating to social studies standards (Harmon, 2000).

> **Research has confirmed that the development of vocabulary is integral to literacy skills.**

Scott, Noel and Asselin (2003) did a comprehensive study on vocabulary instruction in 23 ethnically diverse classrooms. They coded 18,503 minutes of classroom interactions including 9,542 minutes during literacy instruction. They recorded every instance in which word-level knowledge was a focus of instruction, regardless of whether the teacher identified it as vocabulary instruction. Interactions between the teacher and students targeting word knowledge were studied across subject disciplines. They recorded instances of word analysis, appreciation of words as tools for communication and learning specific words.

Then they analyzed the amount of time spent on word learning. They found that only 6% of classroom time was centered on vocabulary development. Of this 6%, only 1.4% was spent on developing word knowledge in core subject areas. Words were most often taught in isolation rather than in context. There was no interdisciplinary relationship between words targeted for study.

The study further defined how the 6 percent of classroom interactions were focused on vocabulary development by using the taxonomy developed by Watts (1995). Vocabulary instruction was divided in five broad categories:

1. *Definitional*: description or statements on a word's meaning

2. *Contextual*: figuring out words from context

3. *Organizational*: organizing words in a semantic framework

4. *Structural*: figuring out word meaning based on morphological structure, prefixes and suffixes, etc.

5. *Mnemonic*: remembering the word by linking key words with visual images

Across the 23 classrooms studied, definitional instruction was most commonly used. Typically, the teacher asked students to look up the definitions of words in the dictionary. Definitional instruction was found in 39% (of the overall 6%) of interactions that targeted word study. The large amount of time focused on this type of instruction for vocabulary acquisition of new words was said to be ineffective (Scott, et al., 2003).

> **Definitional instruction was most commonly used to teach words. Typically, the teacher asked students to look up the definitions of words in the dictionary.**

Several researchers confirm Scott and her associates' evaluation on the ineffectiveness of definitions alone to teach word meanings. They state that looking up word definitions as the unitary way of learning the meanings of words is an inefficient use of students' effort. This technique was noted to be particularly unhelpful for students who know little about the words before this activity (McKeown, 1993; Watts, 1995).

Contextual instruction was teachers' favorite way to present word knowledge. It may be noted that it was also the primary method used by basal language arts texts to instruct students in word study. Context was used in 78% of the total interactions targeted on word development (Scott et al., 2003).

According to Graves (1986), the technique of figuring out unknown word meaning in sentences has been shown to be beneficial when students are instructed to use the following eight context clue types:

1. *Temporal*: duration or frequency; the time element in the surrounding text

2. *Spatial*: location of the unknown word, or the place where the unknown word can be found

3. *Value*: the worth of the unknown word, or how the unknown word affects the reader or the words around it

4. *Descriptive*: any properties, such as size, shape, color, odor, feel, of the unknown word

5. *Functional*: purpose, descriptive actions, or potential uses of the unknown word

6. *Causal*: causes or conditions of the unknown word

7. *Class membership*: class to which the unknown word belongs, or other members of a class of which the word is a member

8. *Equivalence*: meanings, definitions, or synonyms of the unknown word, or antonyms.

Although the eight context clue types are shown to be effective in teaching new vocabulary, students were given little or no instruction on these clues.

> **Contextual instruction was teachers' favorite way to present word knowledge. It may be noted that it was also the primary method used by basal language arts texts to instruct students in word study.**

The practice of figuring out word meaning from the context in which words are embedded can also be highly problematic when it is the only method used for vocabulary development. Research studies have shown that deciphering words from the naturally occurring context can be misleading (Baldwin, 1986). Context alone does not assist students in learning conceptually difficult words that require them to learn a network of new concepts (Nagy, et al., 2000).

Additionally, a study that researched the acquisition of word meaning from context by fifth-grade students of high and low ability found that there was a definite difference between proficient and struggling readers. The proficient readers were significantly better at identifying the correct meaning of a word in context (McKeown, 1985). This was due to the fact that these students had more extensive vocabularies in the first place. Struggling readers often did not even comprehend the other words in the sentence needed to infer meaning.

Teaching words through an organizational approach was defined as students using semantic frameworks or word webs to decipher word meanings. This type of teaching was used in 46% of the 6% of instructional time. While this approach has value in that students learn the interrelationships of concepts associated with the words, the downside is that students must understand the general concepts associated with the words (Scott et al., 2003). Students must learn these new concepts in order for vocabulary development to be truly effective. Therefore, this method of word knowledge is best used in combination with other methods of vocabulary development.

Context alone does not assist students in learning conceptually difficult words that require them to learn a network of new concepts.

A structural approach is used when the focus is on the morphological structure of words, such as prefixes and suffixes. This approach identifies cognates and relationships between words, such as paleontology with archaeology (Fillmore, 2000). Targeting word structure occurred 11% of the time on the interaction coding in the 23 classrooms.

There is a considerable amount of research that confirms the value of a structural approach, especially used in combination with other word learning strategies.

One study on middle school students demonstrated that teaching as few as 20 prefixes and roots improved students' understanding of word meaning and comprehension across subject areas (Harmon, 2005). Although this method has been shown to be valuable from elementary school to high school, it was used very infrequently by classroom teachers in the 23 classes in the Scott et al.'s research study.

Finally, mnemonic instruction was documented as students' attention to remembering a word by linking it to a visual image. A picture of an old woman driving a car might be used to remember the definition of *carlin* (Scott, 2003). This method was used 1% of the time. This is despite the rich literature that supports this technique for learning vocabulary. Mnemonics as a method has the largest amount of data supporting its efficacy; there is little doubt that it works well. Using mnemonics to gain word knowledge is categorized by the literature as a generative process. Students create their own meaning through visual illustrations or word associations. The key word association method facilitates this process.

The following chart summarizes the amount of time devoted to each of the methods of vocabulary development used in the classroom study on vocabulary (Scott, et al., 2003).

Vocabulary Instruction Types	Number of Minutes
Definitional *dictionary* *textbook*	431.5
Contextual *picture* *sentence* *passage*	865.0
Semantic *semantic maps*	515.0
Categorization *semantic features* *synonyms and antonyms*	28.5
Structural *prefixes* *Latin and Greek roots*	130.5
Mneumonic *word associations*	1.0

Overall, the study found that there was little discussion of words. Morphological and contextual analysis were the main strategies that teachers used during the 1.4% of the day devoted to word study in the core subject areas. There were few classrooms where vocabulary was acknowledged as an important part of learning. Students were not immersed in word learning in core subjects, not even in literacy instruction.

Scott et al.'s study clearly reveals the paucity of vocabulary instruction in the core content areas. It affirms data on vocabulary instruction from studies that have been conducted over the last 88 years. The focus on interdisciplinary word study is even more rarely documented in classroom practice, although the research confirms that skills like prefixes and roots help students across subject areas.

The Need for Interdisciplinary Vocabulary Instruction

The need for instruction in content vocabulary from elementary to high school has been clearly documented (Harmon, et al., 2005). There is a definite relationship between the lack of insufficient vocabulary knowledge and students' ability to read and comprehend core content texts (Armbruster and Nagy, 1992). Furthermore, the dearth of instructional support for vocabulary in core textbooks corresponds to students' inability to read these materials (Harmon, 2000).

There is a definite relationship between the lack of insufficient vocabulary knowledge and students' ability to read and comprehend core content texts.

Researchers describe effective instructional practice for teaching vocabulary in the content areas as both subject-related and inter-subject-related. This suggests that it is important for the teacher to instruct students in the interrelationships between and among words (Nagy, 1988). The focus needs to be on the words students need to comprehend core texts and subject concepts.

Think of the words that are integral to the study of mathematics. Researchers have found a direct correlation with knowledge of technical math terms and the success of students in learning math concepts (Gulatt, 1987). Yet, math instructors spend less than 1% of their time on teaching terms.

Vocabulary learning has been deemed particularly critical in math because this content area has more concepts per word, per sentence, per paragraph than any other content area (Harmon, 2005). Students must understand math terms as well as a large number of interdisciplinary words to understand math concepts. For example, consider the following sentence taken from a high school math textbook: *The absolute value of a number is the distance it is from zero.* Students must understand the concept of absolute value, but they also have to be familiar with the interdisciplinary word *distance* to make heads or tails out of this statement.

There are no less than four categories of mathematical terms including: technical, subtechnical, general and symbolic (Monroe, 1995). *Trapezoid* and *rational number* represent mathematical concepts that have one meaning. Subtechnical words are the interdisciplinary words that have multiple meanings like *volume* and *degrees*. Symbolic words include abbreviations like *oz.* for *ounce*. Students must learn words across categories to be able to deal with the cognitive demands of learning mathematics.

The heavy load of technical terms in science texts impedes readability. Science teachers like math teachers, however, spend less than 1% of instructional time on building subject-related and interdisciplinary vocabulary words. Studies have concluded that students' lack of understanding of interdisciplinary words like *component, consistent, exclude* and *interpret* impedes their understanding of science concepts (Marshall, 1991).

One might think that social studies teachers would spend time teaching words that relate to the study of history, geography and government. This is not the case. Although the time spent on vocabulary instruction was more than that in math and science, it amounted to about 3% of instructional time.

Researchers have noted that lack of instruction in geography vocabulary terms has created a generation of learners without map skills. Furthermore 80% of middle school and high schools students were unable to define terms that

> *Vocabulary learning has been deemed particularly critical in math because this content area has more concepts per word, per sentence, per paragraph than any other content area.*

were part of textbook glossaries. An analysis of the glossaries in five social studies textbooks across grade levels revealed that 71% of the terms contained meaningful affixes and roots (Ruff, 1990). This was taken by researchers as evidence that instruction in morphological principles along with interdisciplinary vocabulary would help students to understand social science concepts. For example, teachers could teach word parts such as *port* to help students understand social science concepts like *importing* and *exporting*. Teachers could also use semantic maps to show interrelationships of words that relate to concepts, such as racism.

The Need for Systematic Interdisciplinary Vocabulary Instruction

The research in this chapter clearly presents the need for explicit instruction of vocabulary. Studies done across disciplines address the concern that in order for students to understand subject area texts, they must be taught both words with specialized meanings in particular subject areas and also those interdisciplinary words with multiple meanings in different contexts across subject disciplines.

Yet, the research on classroom practice, even in language arts, clearly reveals that building vocabulary is not a priority in most classrooms. This is despite the close correlation between vocabulary knowledge and comprehension of subject area texts. The lack of attention to word knowledge in classroom practice is also significant considering the large numbers of struggling readers and English language learners. All students, in fact, would greatly benefit from a systematic method of vocabulary development that was implemented across subject areas (Cummins, 2000).

Think About Discussion Questions

1. Think about how you learned vocabulary in school. How much time did your teachers spend on teaching you new words? Did you learn vocabulary words only during language arts? What methods did your teachers use to teach vocabulary?

2. Think about how much time you devote to vocabulary development in the subject area or areas you teach. Make a chart to document the percentage of time that you spend teaching vocabulary using each of the five broad categories below. Evaluate your classroom practice. Write a reflection on how you can improve your delivery of vocabulary instruction.

    - Definitional: *description or statements on a word's meaning*
    - Contextual: *figuring out words from context*
    - Organizational: *organizing words in a semantic framework*
    - Structural: *figuring out word meaning based on morphological structure, prefixes and suffixes etc.*
    - Mnemonic: *remembering the word by linking key words with visual images* (Watts, 1995).

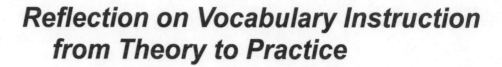

Reflection on Vocabulary Instruction from Theory to Practice

1. Reflect on the research in this chapter that relates to teaching vocabulary in the subject area or one of the subject areas you teach. Analyze how this research would support the following claim: *Students fail to learn subject matter content in a large part due to their limited word knowledge.*

2. Reflect on one of the content standards for the subject or one of the subjects you teach. Identify the subject-specific and interdisciplinary words in the standard. How would you instruct students in these vocabulary words?

Chapter 3

Systematic Interdisciplinary Vocabulary Instruction: A Best Practice

*Systematic vocabulary teaching
has been cited by many
research studies as a Best Practice
for accelerating academic achievement
across subject areas.*

Systematic Interdisciplinary Vocabulary Instruction

The need for vocabulary instruction is based on over eight decades of research that shows consistently that word learning takes place in many steps over time. Systematic teaching is noted to be essential for students' understanding of new words (Paribakhi and Wesche, 1996). The research states explicitly that appropriate attention to vocabulary, based on multiple exposures to words, results in enhanced student achievement. If this is true, then the following two questions should be answered in the affirmative.

1. *Does vocabulary instruction generally result in an increase in students' word knowledge across subject areas?*

> **Students who had received vocabulary instruction significantly outperformed students who did not have the benefit of vocabulary instruction on global vocabulary measures such as standardized tests.**

   The answer to this question is a definite yes. Across studies where outcome tests measured students' knowledge of word definitions (e.g., through sentence anomaly or CLOZE tests), students who had received instruction on the tested words significantly outperformed those who had not. In addition, students who had received vocabulary instruction significantly outperformed the students who did not have the benefit of vocabulary instruction on global vocabulary measures, such as standardized tests. Research studies also demonstrated that vocabulary instruction effectively enhanced learning of words that were not explicitly taught.

2. *Does vocabulary instruction result in an increase in the reading comprehension of students?*

   Again, the answer is yes. Instructed students demonstrated significantly better comprehension of interdisciplinary passages containing taught words than students who were not instructed. More concretely, the students scoring at the 50th percentile on the comprehension of interdisciplinary reading passages were advanced to the level of the 83rd percentile after targeted vocabulary instruction. The instructed students also demonstrated slight but significant gains over their uninstructed peers on standardized measures of reading comprehension, corresponding to an advance from the 50th to the 62nd percentile (Jaeger-Adams, 1996).

If vocabulary instruction leads to increased word knowledge and comprehension across subject areas, then the next question is: *What have we learned about systematic vocabulary development from research?*

Blachowitz and Fisher (2000) have identified the principles upon which systematic vocabulary instruction should be based. These include the following:

- Vocabulary development needs to be an active process where students are engaged in learning words in many ways.

- Discussion of words and their meanings is essential. Students need to be encouraged to make connections between what they know about the concepts the words represent.

- Word learning should be based on multiple sources of information. Students need to manipulate the words across subject areas and explore the meanings of words from several perspectives.

- Vocabulary needs to be personalized. Students need to create their own meaning for words either through illustrations or in writing. Personalizing word meaning helps students learn words more effectively (Fisher and Danielson, 1998). Students internalize these words more easily and develop "vocabulary automaticity."

- Immersion of students in word learning is most important. This means students must be engaged in word learning throughout the day. This involves a commitment to vocabulary development across subject areas (Blachowitz and Fisher, 2000).

These principles for learning vocabulary can be further defined by answering the question: *What instructional strategies are most effective for teaching vocabulary?* Stahl (1986) identified three general strategies that correlate with effective vocabulary instruction. These include: the number and type of exposures both visual and auditory, or rehearsal practice opportunities; the analysis of words both contextual and definitional; and the depth of word processing by using elaborated activities.

> ***Stahl identified three general strategies that correlate with effective vocabulary instruction. These include the following:***
>
> ***The number and type of exposures both visual and auditory***
>
> ***The analysis of words both contextual and definitional***
>
> ***The depth of word processing.***

These general strategies were further defined in a five year study of 50 classrooms across grade levels in three urban school districts. Systematic vocabulary instruction found to be most effective in raising student achievement in both word knowledge and comprehension included the following:

- Rehearsal of the word, including developing background information;

- Word analysis, including context clues, semantic mapping, decoding prefixes and suffixes, and root words;

- Deep processing strategies, using both simple and complex elaboration of meaning (Ventriglia, 2008).

Teachers who used these strategies to target vocabulary instruction experienced the largest class gains in both vocabulary and comprehension measures on standardized tests. These teachers had students "spell and say" the words as part of the rehearsal process. They also had students say or recognize the meanings of words.

Teachers facilitated word analysis for students by pointing out phonetic features of words as well as other morphological features including Latin and Greek roots. Students were also encouraged to use context clues to infer word meanings.

Finally, teachers taught deep processing strategies. They had students elaborate and personalize word meaning. They encouraged students to create pictures or visuals of what the words meant to them. Teachers grouped students and asked them to create original stories using the targeted words.

Overall, teachers who provided their students with many targeted interdisciplinary vocabulary learning opportunities experienced the largest gains on high stakes testing not only in language arts but in other subject areas. The number of practice opportunities was found to directly correlate with students' mastery of vocabulary.

Effective instructional techniques provide a multi-modality approach to vocabulary learning. Visual learners create images and sentences that portray word meaning.

Teachers who provided their students with many targeted interdisciplinary vocabulary learning opportunities experienced the largest gains on high stakes testing not only in language arts but in other subject areas.

Auditory learners thrive on the "spell and say" part of the rehearsal process. Kinesthetic learners greatly benefit from the activities that may include music and dance. Logical/sequential learners benefit by exploring patterns in language.

The strategies of: word rehearsal, word analysis and depth of processing provide a systematic method of helping students develop an extensive vocabulary base.

Number and Types of Rehearsal Opportunities

Research confirms that students' mastery of vocabulary is positively affected by the number and types of rehearsal opportunities (Harmon, 2005).

- Having students "spell and say" vocabulary words is one effective method of rehearsal. Physical movement, such as snapping or clapping while spelling a word's letters, enhances brain activity and enables students to learn words more efficiently (Zadina, 2005). Students can spell and say the words as a class activity or as a paired activity with a partner. The rehearsal method follows the "spell, say and snap" with students saying the definition of the word as a group choral response or as a paired response (Ventriglia, 2008).

- The use of multiple visuals for concept words is another research-based rehearsal method. For example, the concept word *sad* can be represented by many visuals. A picture of a lady crying can be interpreted as sad. So can a face with an upside down smile. A dog can look sad in a picture. The concept or meaning of the word *run* can be represented by a child running in a race, as well as an animal running across a field. Concept words like *sad, happy, shoes* and *run* can be represented by various pictures. Students learn concept words better when they are exposed to multiple, rather than just one or two, visual representations (Ventriglia, 2008).

- Multiple meaning words also can be rehearsed through activities that ask students to match a word's written definition to a picture. For example, a picture representing a table can be matched to its definition as a piece of furniture or as a mathematical compilation of numbers.

- Using graphic organizers to engage students in creating synonyms for words is another effective rehearsal method. Learning the synonyms for words and using them to create sentences develops a breadth of vocabulary knowledge.

These rehearsal opportunities can be implemented across subject areas to develop a repertoire of words that can be crosslinked from one subject to another (Ventriglia, 2008).

When an unknown word is encountered by students in the text, it may cause a "bottleneck" in comprehension. This decreases the student's overall ability to construct a meaningful interpretation of the reading passage.

Contextualized and Decontextualized Word Meanings

Students' speed in accessing the meaning of words increases when they are given strategies on how to use context clues to define the meanings of words (Carlo et al., 2004). The following facts are derived from empirical evidence.

- When an unknown word is encountered by students in the text, it may cause a "bottleneck" in comprehension. This decreases the student's overall ability to construct a meaningful interpretation of the reading passage.

- Students who learn to use context clues to derive the meanings of words develop increased comprehension across subject areas.

- Learning words in context increases the students' speed in constructing meaning from a reading passage.

- Decontextualized knowledge of word meaning is also important for students' vocabulary development. Decontextualized vocabulary practice activities engage students in finding synonyms and antonyms for words, creating word maps and word chains, matching words with definitions and CLOZE activities.

Word Analysis Using Both Definitional and Structural Information

There is widespread agreement and a good deal of empirical evidence which confirms that when individual words are taught, they should be taught using methods that use both definitional and structural information (Beck, 2002).

- Definitional information is defined as knowledge of the relationship between the word and other known words, such as a dictionary definition or a synonym of the word. For example, another word for "gift" is "present."

- Structural knowledge is related to the morphological structures of words, such as prefixes, suffixes as well as Greek and Latin roots. Structural knowledge helps students decipher word meaning.

- Vocabulary teaching methods that include both definitional and structural components enable students to master the meaning of words better than through definitions alone.

- The combination of both definitional and structural information produces a rich and deep word knowledge that crosses subject disciplines. This deep word knowledge enables students to comprehend subject matter texts well enough to apply the higher level thinking skills of analysis, synthesis and evaluation.

There is widespread agreement and a good deal of empirical evidence which confirms that when individual words are taught, they should be taught using methods that use both definitional and structural information.

Depth of Processing

Studies of effective vocabulary acquisition have found that students who process information about words more deeply retain them better. Researchers suggest that new vocabulary is learned more effectively by creating extensive connections to known information or through elaborate processing (Anderson and Reder, 2002). The brain is a natural pattern seeker. Words are learned optimally when interdisciplinary connections are made. Depth of processing is effective for vocabulary learning because it requires more mental effort. Students have to think about the words and create their own meanings through:

1. *Association:* Students create an association between a new word and either a definition, a synonym, or a picture.

2. *Comprehension:* Students demonstrate comprehension of a word by generating synonyms or new phrases in a sentence.

3. *Generation:* Students elaborate word meaning by producing a novel response to the word, such as: a visual image of what the word means, writing an original sentence, or restating the definition in their own words. The product can be written or oral. Generative processing demands more of students' mental resources because it is a creative process.

The three successively deeper levels of word processing include the strategies of *Rehearsal, Word Analysis* and *Deep Processing*. These strategies provide a systematic system for vocabulary development that is entitled *The Rule of 3*. This method immerses students in getting to know a word by making interdisciplinary connections and then by creating their own personal meanings. Students' academic achievement is accelerated when words are taught daily using this method, which is further explained in the following chapter.

> **Studies of effective vocabulary acquisition have found that students who process information about words more deeply retain vocabulary better.**

Think About Discussion Questions

1. Analyze the principles for systematic vocabulary development that Blachowitz and Fisher (2000) have identified on page 37. Explain how many of these principles you incorporate daily in your vocabulary teaching. Give at least one example.

    If you are not currently teaching in a classroom explain how you would incorporate these principles to teach vocabulary in one subject area.

2. Evaluate why generative processing of words leads to the greatest gains in students' retention of vocabulary.

Reflection on Increasing Word Knowledge Through Active Learning

1. Reflect upon the brain research that tells us that when we do something such as snapping our fingers as we spell and say the word, more glucose and oxygen goes to the brain and the word is learned better. If we have students "stand up and explain" the meaning of the word to a partner, the word is learned better. Meyer, Jezzard, Adams, and Turner (1995), in a study on the brain and instruction, found movement enhances brain activity. They found that students think better on their feet. Describe how you can make vocabulary learning more active in your classroom.

2. Based on what you read in this chapter, what argument would you use to support the following statement: *Interdisciplinary vocabulary development is most effective when it is implemented systematically through a multimodality method.*

Chapter 4

The Rule of 3

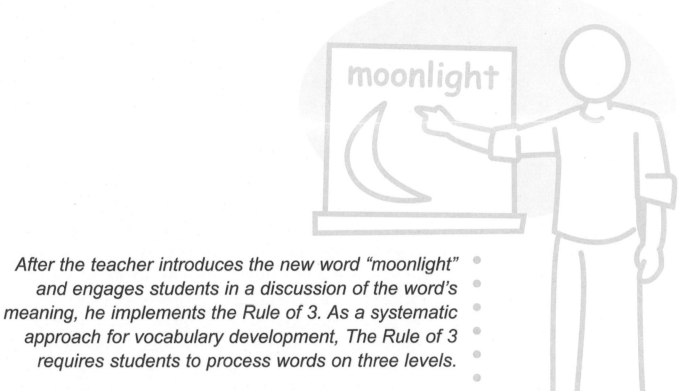

After the teacher introduces the new word "moonlight" and engages students in a discussion of the word's meaning, he implements the Rule of 3. As a systematic approach for vocabulary development, The Rule of 3 requires students to process words on three levels.

The first level of word processing is rehearsal. The teacher has the students spell and say "moonlight" as they snap their fingers or clap out the letters. The teacher gives the definition of the word. Students turn to a partner and give the definition in their own words.

During the second part of the vocabulary development process, the teacher uses word analysis. The teacher emphasizes the phonetic elements of the word. The teacher helps students make a connection between the new word "moonlight" and the other words in the text by emphasizing definitional and contextual information.

At the third and final level of word processing, the teacher has students create a personal representation of the meaning of the word either through a visual or written response.

Systematic Vocabulary Teaching

Did you know that 20 minutes per day of systematic interdisciplinary vocabulary instruction using The Rule of 3 is a proven Best Practice to accelerate word knowledge and reading comprehension across subject areas?

Systematic vocabulary instruction that occurs on a daily basis for the first 10 minutes of class as a warm-up exercise and for the last 10 minutes of class as a review of target vocabulary, results in higher academic achievement. The teaching of 10–15 words a day helps students comprehend core subject texts. Word knowledge contributes to effective oral and written communication across disciplines.

Effective vocabulary teaching includes rehearsal opportunities, word analysis using both definitional and contextual information and depth of word processing using elaboration or production activities. Students need to be given multiple practice opportunities. They need to become engaged in group discussions of words, rather than in filling out ubiquitous worksheets. Vocabulary development to be most valuable must become part of a *Reading Plus Approach* across subject disciplines.

> *The "Reading Plus" approach utilizes vocabulary enhancement activities to improve student vocabulary knowledge and reading comprehension skills.*

"Reading Plus" Approach Vocabulary Acquisition Activities

The "Reading Plus" approach utilizes vocabulary enhancement activities to improve student vocabulary knowledge and reading comprehension skills. It targets *critical words* that are essential for understanding a subject-area or language arts reading passage. Once these critical words are targeted, *The Rule of 3* applies.

The Rule of 3

The key elements for effective vocabulary instruction are incorporated in *The Rule of 3*. The teacher employs at least one activity from each of the three categories:
- Rehearsal
- Word Analysis
- Creative Production

Rehearsal

Mr. Carl Jasper is introducing ten new words to his fifth grade class. He chooses the following critical interdisciplinary words that relate to the social studies lesson he is teaching: adjacent, beneath, border, cautious, descendants, establish, fraction, junction, reasonable, *and* theory. *He first builds background information by conducting a discussion on the meaning of the words. Then he chooses a Rehearsal activity from the Reading Plus Approach: The Rule of 3 (Chart on page 51). He decides to have students* Spell *and* Say *the words and* Write *each word and its meaning. Students spell and say the words in a chant-like manner snapping their fingers. Students repeat the definition of each word chorally with the teacher. They stand up and tell a partner the meaning in their own words. Students finally write each word and a short definition in their Word Journals.*

Mr. Jasper engages students in his class in *Rehearsal* through selective attention to specific words. This first step immerses students in beginning to build word knowledge through the auditory, visual and kinesthetic modality. Vocabulary building at the Rehearsal stage has students recognize new words and actively identify their meanings.

Rehearsal also includes building the background information for word meaning. This includes a discussion of the word in relation to students' experiences. The meaning of *camouflage* to a Vietnamese child may mean the khaki outfits of soldiers; to a Mexican child, it may indicate a man's face hidden under a "*día de los muertos*" mask; to another student, *camouflage* may be the coloring of an animal that blends with the environment.

Miss Rebecca Lemus introduces the following ten critical tier one and tier two interdisciplinary words: again, after, money, prize, basket, before, found, walked, shoes, *and* hand *before teaching the reading lesson and the first-grade English Language Arts standard: Classify grade-appropriate categories of words. She also introduces the idiom* give someone a hand. *After conducting a class discussion on the meaning of the*

Rehearsal also includes building the background information for word meaning. This includes a discussion of the word in relation to students' experiences.

words, she chooses to use Spell and Say and Word Recognition for Rehearsal. Students clap out the letters of the words. They match the words with pictures and then classify words as object concepts, action concepts or time concepts.

A powerful *Rehearsal* technique is to use visuals or pictures that students can match or associate with the meanings of words. There are many places on the Internet where visuals for representations of words can be accessed. A Best Practice is to utilize several pictures to represent a word or concept. The word *shoes* can be best taught by showing pictures of different types of shoes, especially ones that represent a global perspective. The concept of shoes can range from American designer tennis shoes to the clogs used in Holland or the slippers used in China. In fact, the Mandarin word for shoes is synonymous with slippers.

Ms. Marilyn Gonos teaches the subject-specific and interdisciplinary words: genes, DNA, encoded, sequence, organism, specify, amino acids, characteristic, pathway, and prediction before introducing the biology unit on genetics. She targets the words students need to understand the science standard: Genes are a set of instructions encoded in the DNA sequence of each organism that specify the sequence of amino acids in proteins characteristic of that organism. After building background information on the targeted vocabulary words, Ms. Gonos chooses to use Word Recognition as the Rehearsal method. Students match the words to a definition or synonym. Students rehearse by telling the meaning of each word to a partner.

> **A powerful Rehearsal technique is to use visuals or pictures that students can match or associate with the meanings of words.**

Matching words with synonyms is an effective way for students to build vocabulary. By finding synonyms for words, students double their word knowledge. Writing the words and synonyms using vocabulary development activities, such as the ones found in the Activities Section of this book, helps solidify learning.

These three teachers have all chosen one or two ways to accomplish the first step of *The Rule of 3*, Rehearsal. They then choose an activity from the *Word Analysis* column on *The Rule of 3 Chart* (page 51) to immerse students in further word learning.

Word Analysis

Word Analysis engages students in defining target words and using them in context. It focuses student attention on analyzing or manipulating words. Manipulation exercises engage students in arranging, rearranging and organizing words into phrases and sentences. This process draws upon students' knowledge of morphology and grammatical categories. Analyzing words in context requires a deeper level of word processing.

Students need to use interpretation in *Word Analysis*. They use more precise semantic analysis, including the relationship of target words with other words in given contexts (synonyms, antonyms, and classification according to language function). This includes providing information and asking questions using target words.

The fifth grade teacher, Mr. Carl Jasper, chooses *Manipulation* for Word Analysis. He has his students change words from nouns to verbs or from verbs to nouns using their roots. Thus, *descendants,* a noun, is manipulated to become the verb *descend* and *establish*, the verb, is changed to the noun *establishment.*

The first-grade teacher, Miss Rebecca Lemus, focuses on *Phonological Features* for Word Analysis. She asks students to identify beginning and ending sounds of words as well as vowel sounds. By choosing this aspect of Word Analysis, she also reinforces the first-grade English language arts standard: *Distinguish initial, medial and final sounds in single-syllable words.*

The high school teacher, Ms. Marilyn Gonos, chooses *CLOZE Exercises* for Word Analysis. She has her students derive meaning of words in various contexts that relate to the science standard and the study of genetics. For example using the word *encoded: Genes are a set of instructions _____ in the DNA sequence. The _____ proteins are in the influenza virus.*

Word Analysis engages students in defining target words and using them in context. It focuses student attention on analyzing or manipulating words.

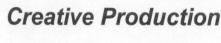

Creative Production

Creative production exercises require recall and reconstruction of words. These exercises involve deep processing of vocabulary. Creative production exercises require the learner to retrieve and produce the target word in appropriate novel contexts. Students may be asked to:

- write their own definition of a word

- draw a picture and write a sentence describing the word's meaning

- answer a question using the target word

- find an idiom misused in a sentence and correct it

   Each of the three teachers ends their vocabulary development with a *Creative Production* activity. These are generative activities in which students create their own personalized meaning for words. Mr. Jasper has students draw a picture and write a sentence for each word in their word journals. Miss Lemus has her first graders write the target words and draw a picture for each word. Ms. Gonos has students use a pictorial representation for each scientific term. Students attach a short word definition to each visual.

   By using at least two of the activities from *Rehearsal*, *Word Analysis* and *Creative Production*, students become immersed in word knowledge. As vocabulary development becomes a part of the classroom routine, it can be done quickly. The *Creative Production* activities can also be assigned as homework.

   The table on page 51 has activities for the *Reading Plus Approach* applying *The Rule of 3*. Accelerated students' reading comprehension across subject areas results from interdisciplinary vocabulary instruction targeting each of the three identified categories. Since practice opportunities are key to vocabulary acquisition, *The Rule of 3 times 3* applies. Students that perform three activities from each of the categories most frequently master targeted interdisciplinary vocabulary.

Reading Plus Approach: The Rule of 3

I. Rehearsal

A. Building Background Information
The student relates the word to his or her own experiences.

B. Spell and say
Students spell and repeat the words several times in a chant-like manner while snapping their fingers or clapping out the letters.

C. Word Recognition
The student chooses the correct picture after seeing or hearing the word.

The student matches the word with its definition or synonym.

The student recognizes the definition of the word from a multiple-choice selection.

D. Writing the Word and its Meaning
The student writes the word and its meaning.

E. Cumulative Recognition
The student uses spell and say with a partner to practice the word. One student says the word and its meaning; the other student writes the word.

F. Self Testing
The student matches words to their meanings.

II. Word Analysis

A. Phonological Features
The student decodes words, blends word parts and identifies letter patterns, root words, suffixes and prefixes and word families such as unwrap, wrap, wrapping, and wrapped.

B. Semantic Mapping
The student constructs a word map.

C. Contextual Meaning
The student derives word meaning in various contexts. He or she writes sentences from the book where the word is found.

The student identifies prefixes and suffixes and Latin and Greek word roots in the context of a reading.

D. Manipulation
The student changes the grammatical category of the word from noun to adjective, verb to noun, or noun to adverb using stems and affixes. Example: independence; independently

E. Classification
The student classifies words according to their discourse function (e.g., cause and effect, contrast)

F. CLOZE Exercises
The student uses words in CLOZE exercises.

III. Creative Production (Deep Processing)

A. Creates Visual Representation
The student creates a visual representation of the word.

B. Construction of Meaning
The student constructs a sentence using the word and writes a definition.

C. Cooperative Grouping
The student works in a group to clarify word meaning through an activity such as "Word and Concept." The group takes a word similar to "endangered" and then applies the word to a concept such as "endangered animals."

D. Mnemonic Strategies
The student employs a mnemonic procedure such as the keyword technique. The keyword technique involves thinking of a word or picture that clues the learner to the meaning of the word.

E. Complex Use of Context
The student derives word meaning from several contexts suggesting alternative words to use in the contexts.

Classroom Setting Factors

The two classroom setting factors that have an effect on vocabulary learning and comprehension are: 1) whether instruction is largely individual or done in a group setting, and 2) the amount of time allocated to instruction. Research has shown that more active processing including discussion of word meaning by students results in higher vocabulary retention. Barron compared vocabulary instruction with and without discussion and found significantly greater word learning with class discussion. Worksheets produced less retention of vocabulary. This is because worksheets were completed individually and were followed by little discussion or direct application to the reading context. Anderson found that students can be very adept at completing worksheets without giving much thought to the content that the teacher intended to cover. Students learned information significantly better when worksheets were completed with a partner (Anderson, 2002).

Researchers found that students can be very adept at completing worksheets without giving much thought to the content that the teacher intended to cover.

Classroom research related to the amount of time spent on vocabulary instruction found that when teachers spent at least 15 to 20 minutes a day on direct vocabulary instruction, student standardized test scores for vocabulary and reading comprehension improved across subject areas.

Think About Discussion Questions

1. Think about *The Rule of 3*. Evaluate why employing at least one activity from each category would improve students' vocabulary acquisition and comprehension in the content subject area or content subject areas that you teach.

2. Create two creative production vocabulary exercises that you could use with a subject area you teach.

Reflection on Vocabulary Learning

1. Reflect upon what you have read in this chapter in relation to class setting factors and the efficiency of group versus individual practice. Evaluate how computer-based activities offer another perspective.

2. Brain research indicates that words are learned better by building connections from the left to the right hemisphere. The right hemisphere uses images such as drawing a picture, metaphor, music, visualizing letters and drama, including spelling out the letters of a word using the right elbow or the hip. The left hemisphere uses language. Describe some vocabulary building activities that would activate both hemispheres.

Chapter 5

English Language Learners and Vocabulary Development

The process of abstracting meaningful concepts and labeling them in a second language can be facilitated through classroom instruction that:

1. Presents English words with concrete objects or pictures

2. Organizes vocabulary into units, grouping words by concepts

3. Expands vocabulary words in a meaningful context

4. Utilizes all the senses in teaching vocabulary

5. Includes mind maps and graphic organizers

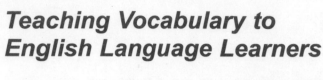

Teaching Vocabulary to English Language Learners

English language learners need social and academic language proficiency to be successful in school (Gottlieb, 2003). Social language proficiency consists of the words needed to engage in social interactions and conversations. Students use social language for greetings. They use such attention getters as, "Hi," "Excuse me," and "How are you doing?" to make and maintain relationships with English speakers.

Knowledge of the English language is gained as students practice using English in social settings. By trying out newly acquired vocabulary in social encounters, English learners come to understand implicitly what language forms fit best in various interactions.

> *Multiple meaning words are some of the most troublesome words for English learners. This is especially true for English learners who do not have multiple meaning words in their native language.*

Along with social language proficiency, English learners must acquire academic words. Academic language proficiency requires the mastery of subject-specific and interdisciplinary words. Multiple meaning words are part of the interdisciplinary vocabulary that students must learn. Students must decipher word meanings according to their use in a subject discipline. For example, the word *degree* referring to temperature in a science text is very different from the word *degree* in a social studies text that refers to a diploma.

Multiple meaning words are some of the most troublesome words for English learners (Calderon, 2004). This is especially true for English learners who do not have multiple meaning words in their native language. It is also true for students who come to school with a very limited vocabulary. They know only one meaning for simple words. This meaning may have nothing to do with how a word is used in a subject-area text. English learners need to learn the multiple meanings of simple words, such as *trunk, steps, ring, seep* and *graph* across subject areas (A list of multiple meaning words can be found on pages 221-222).

Teachers can help English language learners master academic vocabulary including multiple meaning words by: presenting English words with concrete objects or pictures, organizing vocabulary into units, grouping words around concepts, expanding words in meaningful contexts, utilizing all the senses in teaching vocabulary, using graphic organizers and engaging English learners in vocabulary building games.

Present English words with concrete objects or pictures.

Presenting words with their referents, pictures, or concrete objects allows students to tie English words to their conceptual understanding of the words in their first language. This is a bridging process where word labels in English are attached to known concepts.

Group words by concepts.

Grouping words by concepts into a multidisciplinary unit presentation develops and expands vocabulary across content areas. A multidisciplinary unit presentation focused on health and nutrition can be adapted across grade levels by adjusting the activities.

Presenting words with their referents, pictures or concrete objects allows students to tie English words to their conceptual understanding of the words in their first language. This is a bridging process where word labels in English are attached to known concepts.

The unit can commence by having younger English language learners choose pictures of foods they like to eat. Older learners can be asked to survey five members of the class on their favorite foods. The results of the survey can be used to build a table putting students' multicultural food choices into the food pyramid groups developed by the United States Department of Agriculture. English learners should be encouraged to think about where their ethnic foods fit on the food pyramid. For example, tortillas and brown rice would be categorized on the pyramid as breads and grains.

Math applications in this unit can range from comparing and contrasting food calories and portions that students eat to recommended food pyramid choices. Measurement vocabulary is learned as words are introduced that relate to food servings like *scoop, portion, cup, ounce* and *slice*.

Fractions can also be taught in relation to the optimum servings of food recommended by doctors and health professionals. Counting numbers of calories and the percentage of vitamins in foods also has math applications. English learners can compare and contrast calories and vitamins per serving in packaged foods versus fresh foods. Even algebra concepts and statistical probability can be integrated as students estimate the likelihood of becoming overweight or getting diabetes based on dietary habits.

Science applications and science-related vocabulary are weaved into this unit as students learn about the effects of nutrients on the body. WebQuests and online research can be used to lead students to discover the importance of calcium for the optimum functioning of the heart, muscle and nerves. English learners can use their research to analyze and evaluate why over half of Americans do not get the recommended calcium from their normal diets.

Expand vocabulary words.

Nutrition unit words can be expanded in language arts by having students identify the parts of speech. Food products and their descriptions can be labeled as nouns, verbs, adjectives and adverbs. Adjectives that describe foods such as leafy lettuce, spicy Mexican menudo, Asian sticky rice, Hawaiian barbecued beef and crunchy Cuban tostones can be added to students' vocabulary. Adverbs that describe how foods are grown including organically or naturally are also related vocabulary additions.

Social science applications may include having students research the history of global foods. Beginning or Early Production students can match foods to the continents on which they are grown. Intermediate students can be challenged to use Internet links to document the history of rice from a multicultural perspective. Advanced learners can be directed to investigate the history of global food trade through the use of texts and links on the World Wide Web. All these activities expand the words English learners can comprehend and use effectively.

Utilize all the senses in teaching vocabulary.

A multisensory or multimodality approach facilitates word learning for English learners. A multidisciplinary unit on nutrition lends itself to tactile and visual applications. Students can visually describe real fruit and vegetables by size, shape and color. They can also describe the items by touch using words such as *soft, smooth, rough, prickly* or *sticky*. Tasting cooked or uncooked foods further expands vocabulary through the use of words that include *sour, sweet, crunchy, raw, cooked* and *spicy*.

Engage in vocabulary building games and activities.

Interdisciplinary unit presentations for elementary, middle and high school students can be supplemented by vocabulary games. Oral and written language proficiencies are developed through game activities. Food Bingo is an excellent way for beginning language learners to learn the names of food items along with appropriate chunks of language. Students can learn to use chunks or phrases like *I want a_____* or *Give me the_____.*

Parts of speech can be tied to a game of Food Bingo for intermediate language learners. Students can be required to use adjectives to describe food items. Categorization is also an appropriate activity for intermediate students. Food items can be put in groups by description, function or usage. Students can also categorize foods on the food pyramid under grains, fruit, vegetables or dairy products.

A game for upper elementary, middle school or high school English learners utilizes pictures from supermarket brochures or Internet advertisements.

Students are grouped in pairs and given three food related advertisements. The goal of the game is to have students identify the advertised products by asking questions such as: *Do you buy this product cooked or uncooked? Is it served for dessert or the main course?* The sophistication of the questions will depend on the student's level of language proficiency. This game is very powerful for all levels of English learners because it develops the skill of questioning or the heuristic function of language.

Multimedia game applications and WebQuests also help students master academic language. Games on the World Wide Web often have links that translate words. This is helpful for beginning language learners. Some Web-based applications to disciplines like science and math also give students concept translation options. These options allow students to process concepts in their own language until they gain at least a level of intermediate proficiency in English.

> *Multimedia game applications and WebQuests also help students master academic language. Games on the World Wide Web often have links that translate words. This is helpful for beginning language learners.*

Use mind maps and graphic organizers.

The use of mind maps and graphic organizers facilitate the learning of vocabulary for English learners. Graphic organizers range from simple word maps that can be used by elementary students to more sophisticated graphic organizers for upper elementary, middle school and high school students. Words can be grouped around interdisciplinary concepts. Word webs can be utilized by more advanced learners to extend vocabulary words to synonyms and antonyms.

vegetables — whole grains — *healthy* foods — fruit

devour — consume — *synonyms* eat — ingest

Brainstorming for Academic Vocabulary Building

Brainstorming is an effective technique that can be integrated in unit presentations to develop academic vocabulary. The Brainstorming strategy is validated by research that states that words are remembered best when they are tied to students' cultural or experiential background knowledge. New vocabulary words are best expanded from these vantage points (Myers, 1996).

The strategy of *Brainstorming* can be used to begin a unit on global communication. Students can be asked to brainstorm with a partner everything they know about communication. It is these known concepts that then become the basis for building academic vocabulary for English learners. For example, if English learners use the words sending email messages, these words can be expanded to texting messages and faxing messages.

Word linking using a graphic organizer is a Brainstorming strategy that develops word knowledge for English learners. Vocabulary is expanded as paired students "brainstorm" related words on a topic like global communication. Students link words together one after another on a graphic organizer. Older English learners can make use of a thesaurus in text form or online to find related words. An example of a word linking graphic organizer follows. This graphic organizer can be found in the Activities Section of Chapter 7 on page 201.

> *The Brainstorming strategy is validated by research that states that words are remembered best when they are tied to students' cultural or experiential background knowledge. New vocabulary words are best expanded from these vantage points.*

Start Here communication	cell phone	email	fax

Sequencing is a variation of the technique of word linking. Instead of linking words, concepts are linked in sequential order. This technique can be used for retelling a story with pictures indicating what happened first, next and last. Sequencing items on language proficiency tests are among the most difficult for English learners. The strategy of sequencing can be learned by students when it is reinforced across disciplines. Students can sequence the steps to solving a math problem or the procedures in a science experiment. They can also sequence in chronological order what they learned about the events in World War II.

Nonlinear learning encourages brainstorming because students decide what links they will use to expand their knowledge. Brainstorming encourages students to use language for its highest function which is creation.

There are multimedia applications of the brainstorming technique of sequencing. Upper elementary, middle school and high school students can explore a topic through links on the World Wide Web. The information gleaned from these links can be sequenced in chronological order or in another creative way. Nonlinear learning encourages brainstorming because students decide what links they will use to expand their knowledge. Brainstorming encourages students to use language for its highest function which is creation.

Research on the Development of Academic Vocabulary for English Learners

Along with the preceding suggestions and activities for the development of academic vocabulary, there are research studies that discuss techniques and groupings. A research study by Thomas and Collier (2002) found that English learners acquired academic vocabulary better when they were not segregated by level of English language proficiency. Students learned better in mixed ability groups.

Thomas and Collier also noted that cognates should be taught to English learners. *Cognates* are words that look the same in two languages and have the same meaning. Some cognates in Spanish are *fruta* (fruit) and *familia (family)*.

Students can also be taught parts of speech as they learn cognates. Cognates include all parts of speech ranging from verbs like *abandonar* (abandon) to nouns like *camello* (camel). A list of cognates can be found on pages 218-220.

There are 10,000 to 15,000 words in Spanish that are cognates. This means that if Spanish speakers know the meaning of these words in Spanish, they can easily bridge the meaning to the English words. This quickly gives Spanish speakers a large English vocabulary.

It is important, however, when teaching cognates to remember there are also false cognates. *False cognates* are words that look the same in English and Spanish but have different meanings. Some false cognates are *rope/ropa* and *embarrassed/embarasada*. The word *ropa* does not mean *rope* in Spanish. It means *clothing*. The word *embarasada* does not mean *embarrassed* in Spanish. It means *pregnant*. Other words that look like words in English but mean something different in Spanish are *recordar* (remember), *vaso* (glass), *carpeta* (folder), *parientes* (relatives), *realizar* (to make, to actualize) and *soportar* (to put up with).

Another study on academic vocabulary instruction conducted by Calderon (2004) documented the effects of systematic instruction. In Calderon's study, English learners were taught 10 to 20 words a week from textbooks. Words were presented with concrete representations, pictures, pantomime and gestures. The words then were used in activities and games after reading. Teachers also used CLOZE strategies to help English learners to derive meaning from context.

Calderon had an experimental group of English learners who received vocabulary instruction and a control group who received no instruction. The group who received direct vocabulary instruction not only increased their mastery of academic vocabulary words, but also increased their proficiency on word attack and comprehension skills.

> **There are 10,000 to 15,000 words in Spanish that are cognates. This means that if Spanish speakers know the meaning of these words in Spanish, they can easily bridge the meaning to the English words. This quickly gives Spanish speakers a large English vocabulary.**

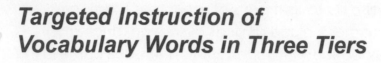

Targeted Instruction of Vocabulary Words in Three Tiers

Calderon grouped vocabulary words for targeted instruction in three tiers: basic words, interdisciplinary words and subject specific words. English learners were taught words that corresponded to their language proficiency levels. Early production students were taught tier one words including cognates, as well as some interdisciplinary tier two words. Intermediate and advanced English learners were taught tier two and tier three words, including multiple meaning words.

Calderon found that directly teaching tier one and tier two words had a significant impact on the reading comprehension of English learners across subject areas. Vocabulary instruction, emphasizing tier two words, resulted in a significant increase in English learners' comprehension of content texts.

Calderon noted that word knowledge and reading comprehension are intricately connected for English learners. The achievement gap in reading performance between English only students and English learners has been found to be directly related to gaps in vocabulary knowledge. Calderon's research proved that systematic vocabulary development helps to close this achievement gap (Calderon, 2004).

It is worth noting that Calderon categorized certain idioms, everyday expressions, and proverbs as tier two vocabulary. Phrases such as "once upon a time," "all walks of life," "the meat of the issue," "to face," and "melting pot" need to be taught explicitly. Native English speakers take these phrases for granted, and many of these phrases are unique to English-speaking cultures. (A list of idioms can be found on pages 223-225).

Targeting vocabulary and repeated usage are important for English learners. In literature written for native English speakers, for example, vocabulary is varied.

> *The achievement gap in reading performance between English only students and English learners has been found to be directly related to gaps in vocabulary knowledge. Calderon's research proved that systematic vocabulary development helps to close this achievement gap.*

The same word is not repeated; synonyms and other word choices are used. This avoidance of recycling, which results in more interesting literature, does a disservice to English learners. Students who are not proficient in English benefit from the recycling of vocabulary within the same story, and from reading selection to selection. English learners need these multiple exposures to master new vocabulary.

A study by Carlo, August, and Snow et al. (2004) addressed the challenge of closing the achievement gap in reading by addressing the vocabulary needs of English learners in bilingual and mainstream classrooms. An intervention was designed to enhance the academic vocabulary of fifth-graders. The intervention consisted of teaching academically useful words together with strategies for using information from context, from morphology and from cognates to infer word meaning. The study's major goal was to test the impact of a vocabulary enrichment intervention on English learners and English only students.

The results of the research studies revealed that the explicit or direct teaching of vocabulary accelerated word-learning and increased comprehension across subject areas for both English learners and English only students. The researchers noted that the most important principles for systematic vocabulary teaching include: word knowledge involving spelling and pronunciation, morphology and syntax and depth of word meaning. These principles are referred to in this Best Practice book as *The Rule of 3*. *The continued use of these principles was shown to accelerate students' vocabulary development.*

Research clearly supports the teaching of academic vocabulary for English learners. Systematic teaching of vocabulary results not only in increased word knowledge but also in higher levels of reading comprehension.

Research clearly supports the teaching of academic vocabulary for English learners. Systematic teaching of vocabulary results not only in increased word knowledge but also in higher levels of reading comprehension. Therefore, using a systematic approach, such as the *Rule of 3* ensures that English learners will master the academic vocabulary needed for success in school and in the greater community.

The Rule of 3

Develops Vocabulary for English Learners

I.   Rehearsal: "Spell and Say"
- Build background information on the word.
- Spell and say the word clicking out its letters.
- Tell the meaning of the word to a partner.

II.   Word Analysis
- Use phonetic and context clues to help derive word meaning.
- Create a semantic word map.

III.   Creative Production: Deep Processing
- Do a creative activity with the word.
  Draw a picture. Write a sentence or story.
- Create word relationships.

Think About Discussion Questions

1.   Cognates are words that are similar in both English and another language.

     Analyze the list of Spanish and English language cognates that are on pages 218-220.

     Make a list of the cognates that would help English learners master the subject area or one of the subject areas you teach.

2.   Create two brainstorming activities for English learners that relate to the subject area you teach or one of the subject areas you teach.

Reflection on Developing Vocabulary for English Learners

1. Reflect upon a recent report issued by the California Commission of Teacher Credentialing that stated: *Teachers need to be provided with effective methods and more advanced levels of knowledge on how to work with English learners. There are large numbers of students that remain at the intermediate level of English proficiency and never advance to full proficiency.* Create a solution to this issue based on the research presented in this chapter.

2. Create or find a game on the Internet that would help English learners master the vocabulary related to the subject area(s) you teach.

Chapter 6

Vocabulary Development: English Language Arts Standards and Instructional Practices

English Language Arts Standards reflect the need for vocabulary development across grade levels. Research suggests that along with phonemic awareness and decoding activities, vocabulary development is key to success in reading across content areas.

English Language Arts Standards

The English language arts standards target vocabulary and concept development under the category of Word Analysis, Fluency and Systematic Vocabulary Development. The standards for vocabulary development build upon each other from grade level to grade level. Thus, the kindergarten standard of *describing common objects* sets the foundation for the third grade vocabulary standard of *demonstrating knowledge of specificity among grade-appropriate words.* The mastery of vocabulary standards at each grade level is important for student success in reading.

> **The importance of vocabulary development is acknowledged by the research which states that after English learners and struggling readers master decoding skills, lack of vocabulary skills remain the chief barrier for success in content reading.**

The importance of vocabulary development is acknowledged by the research which states that after English learners *and struggling readers* master decoding skills, lack of vocabulary skills remain the chief barrier for success in *content* reading. It is important for all teachers to understand the sequence in which vocabulary skills are developed through the English language arts standards. Understanding the types of skills students are expected to master enables teachers across subject areas and grade levels to address any gaps in students' vocabulary skills.

English Language Arts Standards for Kindergarten

English language arts standards for kindergarten include:

- Identifying and sorting common words from basic categories (e.g., colors, shapes, foods).

- Describing common objects and events in both general and specific language.

Methodical vocabulary instruction in kindergarten must develop understanding of words and concepts as building blocks of language categories, including color, shape and size. Common procedural and comparative words, such as *underline, group, same* and *different,* must also be directly taught. Vocabulary is developed through direct instruction in kindergarten.

Visuals and manipulatives are important in helping students grasp word meaning. Story reading, including a picture walk to identify and label visuals, expands vocabulary. Listening centers and computer software programs that include matching pictures and concepts also improve word knowledge.

Another kindergarten skill is story retelling. Students gain practice in sequencing words as they retell events in a story. Story retelling is one of the most important language-building activities for young students.

English learners need extensive vocabulary development. They must acquire 5,000 words at the kindergarten level. Students need to bridge English labels to words and concepts that they already know in their first language. This is done most easily through visuals and concrete activities where students can practice words in a meaningful context. Songs, chants and games help kindergarten students learn words. Repetition, including multiple practice opportunities, is key to mastering vocabulary words for kindergarten students.

Vocabulary words critical to listening comprehension need to be taught directly to students. Words learned in oral language activities can be bridged to beginning reading skills, including phonemic awareness activities, such as clapping out the syllables of words or blending sounds.

In summary, factors that accelerate vocabulary development at the kindergarten level include the following:

- Multiple exposure to words

- Target teaching of words that are critical to the understanding of a story or concept

- Target teaching of high utility words

- Deep word processing in multiple contexts

- Use of visuals and manipulatives to clarify word meaning

- Use of *The Rule of 3* to teach vocabulary words

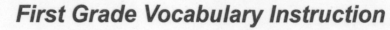

First Grade Vocabulary Instruction

Vocabulary instruction in the first grade should build upon the skills that students have mastered in kindergarten. Activities must extend word meanings and concepts. The English language arts standard at the first grade asks students to:

- Classify grade-appropriate categories of words (e.g., concrete collections of animals, foods and toys).

Classifying is an important activity at the first grade level for all students. Differentiated instruction moves students from their current level of language proficiency to advanced levels of language development. For example, classifying activities for animals can be differentiated by the level of students' language development.

Beginning English learners can classify animals by colors. The next level of learners can group animals by category (e.g., mammals, birds, reptiles and fish). The most sophisticated students can classify animals by habitat or diet (e.g., herbivore, carnivore).

Methodical vocabulary instruction in the first grade focuses on basic categorization of grade-appropriate concepts (e.g., animals, foods, clothing) and the vocabulary words that students need to comprehend content.

> *Differentiated instruction moves students from their current level of language proficiency to advanced levels of language development.*

Vocabulary development occurs through direct instruction of specific words and through exposure to new concepts. Exposure is most important at this level. Students need to learn a broad range of words in different content areas ranging from literature to science.

First grade students need to learn specific vocabulary in context. Learning vocabulary in context facilitates comprehension skills. Direct instruction in vocabulary for first-grade students should involve an integrated approach that uses the listening, speaking, reading and writing of new vocabulary words.

Standards for the Second Grade

Second grade vocabulary standards target the following skills:

- Understanding and explaining common antonyms and synonyms
- Using knowledge of individual words in unknown compound words to predict their meaning
- Knowing the meaning of simple prefixes and suffixes (e.g. *over-, un-, -ing, -ly*)
- Identifying simple multiple-meaning words

Second graders need multiple practice opportunities to master vocabulary. They need exposure to words in various contexts and subject areas. Understanding synonyms and antonyms are new skills introduced in the second grade.

The emphasis on decoding in most core textbooks from kindergarten through second grade often leaves little time for teachers to expand word meanings. At second grade, students must move from simply decoding words to understanding key vocabulary words and using them in written activities.

It is the critical second-grade tier two vocabulary that needs to be learned and then expanded to synonyms. These words can also be taught through reading comprehension and writing activities. Students can be asked to underline words in a simple passage and then replace them with synonyms. Once students master the concept of synonyms, then antonyms can be introduced.

Simple multiple meaning words are another target for vocabulary instruction. Remember that multiple meaning words are particularly difficult for English learners. This is because many of these students speak languages that have specific words to label different objects and parts of speech.

Multiple meaning words and their definitions should be introduced in the second grade with visuals. Students need to learn the usage and definition of these words in the context of a subject discipline. The multiple meaning word *check* can be defined as a money order in language arts and as the verb *check* in mathematics, to look over the answers to problems. The goal is to have students become aware that multiple meaning words must be figured out in context.

Students need to learn multiple meaning words in the context of a subject discipline.

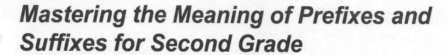

Mastering the Meaning of Prefixes and Suffixes for Second Grade

Understanding the meaning of simple prefixes and suffixes is an important second grade standard. Strategies that facilitate students' learning of prefixes and suffixes include:

- Using multiple exposures to root words including visuals to illustrate the meanings of the words with and without prefixes or suffixes

- Defining the meaning of words with prefixes and suffixes in the context of a sentence or paragraph

- Teaching the meaning of prefixes and suffixes in isolation first; then attaching the prefixes and suffixes to words.

- Reinforcing prefixes and suffixes that appear in sequences of instruction using explanation charts like the one that follows. The chart contains the most important prefixes and suffixes that are to be mastered in the second grade

Grade Two

Base Word	Prefix/Suffix	Meaning	New Word
lock	un-	not	unlock
plant	re-	again	replant
thank	-ful	full of	thankful
home	-less	without	homeless
work	-er	one who does	worker
slow	-ly	in a way that is	slowly
enjoy	-ment	act of	enjoyment
member	-ship	state of	membership
stick	-y	like or full of	sticky

Additional examples: agreement, banker, builder, careful, careless, colorful, deeply, dusty, endless, fearful, friendly, friendship, healthy, hopeful, hopeless, leadership, mighty, movement, painful, painless, quietly, rebuild, refill, remake, rename, reopen, repay, replay, rerun, retell, rewrite, singer, softly, stormy, successful, unable, uncertain, uneven, unfriendly, unhappy, unhealthy, unkind, unwise

Continuing Language Arts Skills
for the Third Grade

Third grade students need multiple exposures to new words through different types of reading, including expository, narrative, functional, and recreational passages. Third-grade students are ready to begin using the dictionary to identify word meanings. Students need practice both with dictionary textbooks and with digital dictionaries like dictionary.com.

One effective strategy requires students to use the dictionary to define targeted words in short passages. Students find the targeted words in the dictionary. They also copy the word in the context of a sentence from the passage. For example, the word *reasonable* can first be looked up in the dictionary. Then the sentence from the text can be read, written and discussed. Discussion of words used in context is a key strategy for mastering words.

Using context to understand the meaning of unfamiliar words is a key strategy that should be taught to third-graders. Teaching students to use context includes helping students to understand that they must use all the words surrounding the unfamiliar word to provide information on its meaning.

Third grade students need to continue to master synonyms, antonyms, prefixes and suffixes. They also need to develop more sophisticated categorization skills. English Language Arts Standards that are targeted for third grade include:

- Using knowledge of antonyms, synonyms, homophones and homographs to determine the meanings of words

- Demonstrating knowledge of levels of specificity among grade-appropriate words and explaining the importance of these relations (e.g. dog/mammal/animal/living things)

- Using sentence and word context to find the meaning of unknown words

- Using a dictionary to learn the meaning and other features of new words

- Using knowledge of prefixes (e.g., *un-, re-, pre-, bi-, mis-, dis-*) and suffixes (e.g., *-er, -est, -ful*) to determine the meaning of words

> *Third grade students are ready to begin using the dictionary to identify word meanings.*

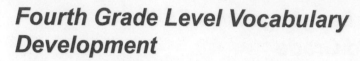

Fourth Grade Level Vocabulary Development

The fourth grade initiates student transition from the primary to the intermediate grades. Vocabulary development at this grade level is closely linked to reading across content areas. English language arts standards for the fourth grade include:

- Applying knowledge of word origins, derivations, synonyms, antonyms and idioms to determine the meaning of words and phrases

- Using knowledge of root words to determine the meaning of unknown words within a passage

- Knowing common roots and affixes derived from Greek and Latin and using this knowledge to analyze the meaning of complex words (e.g., international)

- Using a thesaurus to determine related words and concepts

- Distinguishing and interpreting words with multiple meanings

> **Vocabulary development at this grade level is closely linked to reading across content areas. The standards at this level emphasize synonyms, antonyms, idioms and words with multiple meanings.**

The standards at this level emphasize synonyms, antonyms, idioms and words with multiple meanings. Idioms need to be used repeatedly in context for English learners to grasp their meaning. English learners tend to be very literal. So when an idiom is used such as, *it's raining cats and dogs*, they really expect to see cats and dogs coming down from the heavens. Games help English learners understand the meaning of idioms. (See pages 223–225 for a list of important idioms.)

Synonyms and antonyms can also be taught in game-like activities. Using poetry and short passages to change underlined words to synonyms helps students gain an understanding of how to manipulate words to create a new passage or poem that says the same thing but in different words.

Students can change words in passages or poems by referring to the dictionary or thesaurus. Students at the fourth grade level should become extremely conversant with using the dictionary and thesaurus to research related words and concepts.

Reading short narrative and expository passages helps English learners master vocabulary. The emphasis should be on having students determine the main idea and the author's purpose. Students' focus on vocabulary in expository passages is to understand facts, opinions, sequence and order. Research by Baker et al. (1993) states that students are more successful in reading at this level when the teacher:

- Targets specific tier two vocabulary words that are critical to the comprehension of reading selections

- Teaches concepts and establishes the purpose for the reading selection

- Pre- and post-tests vocabulary words and reading comprehension

- Encourages independent reading of fiction and nonfiction books and articles to increase word knowledge

- Uses the newspaper, menus and other practical materials to develop reading comprehension and vocabulary

- Establishes objectives for each vocabulary activity

- Teaches vocabulary learning strategies, including the use of context clues and CLOZE activities for word substitution

- Gives students multiple exposures to vocabulary words.

Fifth Grade Language Arts Standards

Fifth graders are expected to understand and use language in a more sophisticated manner. They need to understand the use of figurative and metaphorical words in context. They also must begin to utilize root derivatives of Greek and Latin to analyze the meaning of vocabulary words.

The English language arts standards for fifth grade emphasize the use of morphological, etymological and historical word clues. Students need to begin to understand the morphology or the study and description of words, including inflection and derivation. Etymology involves the history of a word. This may include studying its Latin roots or other ancestral forms. Direct instruction of some of the more common Latin word roots is an important instructional strategy at this grade level. The study of figurative language can be developed through poetry and mythology. (See Chapter 7 activities.)

English Language Arts Standards for the fifth grade include:

- Using word origins to determine the meaning of new words

- Understanding and explaining frequently used synonyms, antonyms and homographs

- Knowing abstract, derived roots and affixes from Greek and Latin and using this knowledge to analyze the meaning of complex words (e.g., *controversial*)

- Understanding and explaining the figurative and metaphorical use of words in context

Writing activities develop vocabulary at this grade level. Activities that encourage word association and mind mapping before writing expand student vocabulary.

The strategy titled "Story Impressions" develops vocabulary before the students read a story (McGinley and Denner, 1987). The teacher chooses 5–10 words that are critical to the comprehension of the story. Then the teacher writes the words on the whiteboard and conducts a discussion with students on the meaning of words. Finally, the teacher puts the students in groups. The groups compose a story using the words in the order that they are listed. (This strategy is outlined on page 208.)

Vocabulary Instruction for the Sixth Grade

Sixth grade English language arts standards target word origins, root words and suffixes. They also focus on the interpretation of figurative language and multiple word meanings. Standards for the sixth grade include:

- Identifying and interpreting figurative language and words with multiple meanings

- Recognizing the origins and meanings of frequently used foreign words in English and using these words accurately in speaking and writing

- Monitoring expository text for unknown words with novel meanings by using sentence and paragraph clues

- Understanding and explaining "shades of meaning" in related words (e.g., *softly* and *quietly*)

Systematic vocabulary instruction for the sixth grade should include word analysis. The emphasis should be on the origins of words and multiple word meanings. The thesaurus should be used at this grade level on an ongoing basis. Writing activities should include word substitution in context.

Systematic vocabulary instruction for the sixth grade should include word analysis. The emphasis should be on the origin of words and multiple word meanings.

Vocabulary Instruction for Seventh and Eighth Grades

The English language arts standards for seventh and eighth grades or middle school further develop student knowledge of Greek, Latin and Anglo-Saxon word roots, idioms and analogies. Metaphors are developed through the use of prose and poetry. Students at this level are expected to use context clues to identify word meanings through definition, example and restatement. The English language arts standards for vocabulary development at the seventh and eighth grades include:

- Identifying idioms, analogies, metaphors and similes in prose and poetry

- Using knowledge of Greek, Latin and Anglo-Saxon roots and affixes to understand content and vocabulary

- Clarifying word meaning through definition, example and restatement or contrast

Students at the middle school level are expected to use context clues to identify word meanings through definition, example and restatement.

Middle school students need vocabulary development across content areas. The goal is for students to approach vocabulary development like scientists. They need to become proficient at dissecting words and using Latin and Greek roots to "figure out" word meanings. Middle school students then need to apply the meanings of words in both expository and narrative reading and writing.

Vocabulary Development for High School Students

The vocabulary standards for High School students require them to analyze the meanings of words in relation to the arguments and propositions advanced in interdisciplinary reading in social studies, science, math and language arts textbooks. By grade 12, students are expected to read 2 million words annually, including words from classic works, literature, science, newspapers and online information.

The English language arts standards for vocabulary development in the ninth and tenth grades include:

- Understanding and using literal and figurative meanings of words and understanding word derivations

- Distinguishing between denotative and connotative meaning of words

- Identifying Greek, Roman and Norse mythology and using the knowledge to understand the origin and meaning of new words

The English language arts standards for vocabulary development in the eleventh and twelfth grades include:

- Tracing the etymology of significant terms

- Applying knowledge of Greek, Latin, and Anglo Saxon roots and affixes to draw inferences

- Discerning the meaning of analogies and concepts encountered

- Using graphic organizers like the Venn diagram to compare and contrast concepts

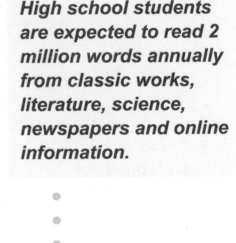

High school students are expected to read 2 million words annually from classic works, literature, science, newspapers and online information.

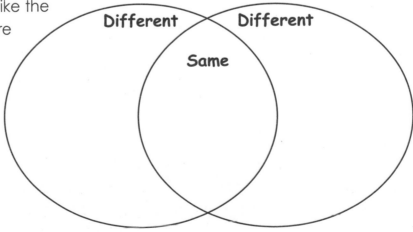

Vocabulary Development and Standards for English Learners

English learners must master English language development standards as well as academic content standards. The teacher's role is to help bridge the two sets of standards. As English learners move up through the grades, the language complexity becomes more and more difficult. English learners must learn to use academic and technical vocabulary to comprehend varying lengths of utterances and reading passages. They must use paralinguistic cues and visual support to construct meaning.

At the beginning level of language proficiency, primary students need to learn vocabulary as well as sentence patterns in English. Students can learn sentence patterns by writing them with vocabulary words. For example, the pattern: *I have a _____.* (e.g., book, computer, pencil).

Intermediate, middle school and high school beginning English learners can acquire sentence patterns by copying sentences that answer questions from the textbook. At the beginning levels of language proficiency, it is much too difficult for students to compose their own sentences. However, they can learn vocabulary by copying sentences from the book and reading the sentences to a partner.

The essential task for English language learners is to recognize the words that are necessary for understanding the essence of a passage, rather than irrelevant specifics.

Most English learners at the intermediate proficiency level face an overwhelmingly large number of unknown words in content textbooks. Vocabulary knowledge is crucial to the comprehension of these interdisciplinary content materials. The essential task for English language learners is to recognize the words that are necessary for understanding the essence of a passage, rather than irrelevant specifics (Cassie, 1990).

Methodical instruction in the parts of speech facilitates the English learner's ability to target the words that are essential for the understanding of a passage.

Once students can identify the parts of speech, they can determine whether a word is essential for basic understanding of the content material. For example, looking up adverbs and adjectives does little to facilitate the understanding of a passage. While adverbs and adjectives add spice to a reading selection, they do not have a serious effect on a sentence's meaning. If students can understand the subject, verb and object, often they have understood the basic meaning of a sentence.

Instruction for English learners in parts of speech must include the learning of word families. English learners need to be instructed in both the meaning and spelling of words that are part of word families.

The English language contains many word families in which the meanings of different parts of speech are not consistent and/or the internal structure of the words is varied. For example, *compelling, compulsion, compulsive, compulsory* are all part of one word family. The teacher should point out similarities among words in word families as well as differences in meaning.

English learners need to understand how changing the spelling of a word by adding a suffix influences the word's meaning and part of speech. When you change the verb perform to performer, the word changes from a verb to a noun. Chapter Seven contains sample worksheets for teaching suffixes and parts of speech.

All vocabulary needs to be introduced at the developmental level of English learners. The chart that follows on page 84 delineates how to target vocabulary development for English learners.

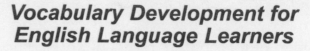

Vocabulary Development for English Language Learners

Words to target in reading selections for
English language learners.

LEVEL ONE: Words with concrete referents

- Words that can be tied to a picture, concrete object or action
- Target 10 words, such as: table (*point to table*)
    hat (*show picture of a hat*)
    run (*perform action*)

 The word should be placed next to the object or picture or next to the student who is performing the action. This enables English learners to make an immediate association.

LEVEL TWO: Words that are critical for the understanding of the text and high frequency words

- Teach these words in a sentence context.
- Identify 8 to 10 of the most important sentences in the subject reading. These should be the sentences students need for comprehension.
- Write these sentences on sentence strips and underline the vocabulary words.
- Have students read and write the sentences.
- Have students draw a picture for each sentence.
- Give students at least 10 exposures to these sentences. For example, ask the students to arrange the illustrated sentences in order (sequence).

LEVEL THREE: Words tied to descriptions of nouns or verbs

- Make a word map using nouns and verbs.
- Make a word chain of descriptors to a noun or verb.
- Change the noun or verb in a sentence.

Methodical Teaching Strategies for English Language Learners

Finally, teaching English learners new vocabulary in context prior to reading a content selection facilitates comprehension. The goal of teaching words in context exercises is to have students form a general understanding of the meaning of unknown words. An example of a vocabulary development exercise using context can be found in Chapter Seven on page 183.

A strategy for teaching English learners vocabulary words embedded in context is the *Recycled Words Strategy*. The Recycled Words Strategy has five stages:

1. Pre-reading activities

2. Oral reading strategies

3. Building vocabulary through focused word study activities

4. Word knowledge assessments

5. Writing workshop (Blake, 1995)

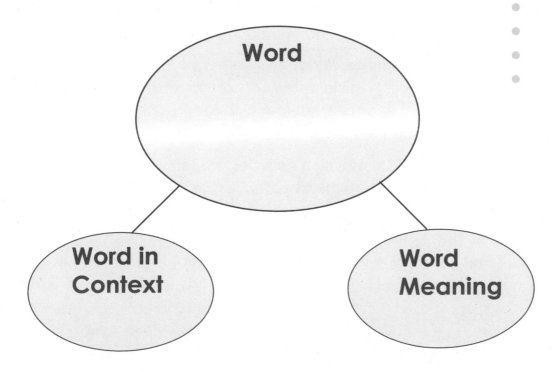

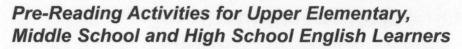

Pre-Reading Activities for Upper Elementary, Middle School and High School English Learners

- The teacher selects target words that are crucial to the understanding of the subject text and presents them to students on the overhead or whiteboard.

- The teacher leads students in the "spell and say" strategy. Students and teachers spell and say targeted words.

- The "Invisible List Strategy" is used by the teacher to reinforce the "spell and say" strategy.

- **Invisible List Strategy:** Students select six to eight of the targeted vocabulary words. The teacher writes the words on the whiteboard and leads the students in reading the list several times. The teacher then starts to erase the words one by one. The students continue to read the list as if the words were still there. They continue reading the now invisible words. The invisible list strategy can also be implemented by writing the vocabulary words on index cards and then removing the index cards one at a time. This activity gives students practice in remembering targeted content vocabulary.

- **Vocabulary Worksheets:** This activity at the pre-reading level has students scan designated sections of the subject text to find words that match the definitions.

- **Multiple Choice Worksheets:** Target vocabulary words are given with possible definitions or synonyms. Students circle the best choice, given their knowledge. The reading of the text validates their choices.

- **Creative Construction Activities:** Students create their own sentences using the target words. Beginning students fill in words in CLOZE sentences and illustrate the sentences.

These pre-reading activities can be implemented across subject areas. Pre-reading activities help students master the vocabulary necessary for the understanding of important subject-area concepts. When students comprehend what they are reading, they can more easily use higher level thinking skills to analyze, synthesize and evaluate what they have read.

Oral Reading Strategies for English Learners

- **Jump-In Reading:** This is an interactive technique. After the teacher has activated prior knowledge and targeted key vocabulary for a selection, one student starts to read. The student stops at any time. Students make a signal to indicate that they have heard one of the targeted words.

- **Checking for Understanding:** The teacher should check after each paragraph for students' understanding of key vocabulary terms. Students need to be asked to identify the meaning of words in the context of the subject selection.

Vocabulary Building through Focused Word Study Activities

- **Color-Coded Index Cards:** These cards provide a systematic way for English learners to acquire word knowledge. Targeted vocabulary from the text is color-coded on 3 x 5 cards. For example, all the words from one subject area selection may be color-coded on yellow cards. Words from another subject area may be color-coded on green cards. The definitions of words are written on the other side of the cards. Students then may mix and match words in writing activities. Students can use the words to write sentences or to compose expository or narrative text. This activity contributes to interdisciplinary vocabulary development.

- **Game Cards:** Two cards are prepared. One card has the target word, sentence and part of speech. The other card has the definition. Students match target words to their definitions.

Word Knowledge Assessments

There are various types of quizzes that help evaluate vocabulary retention. These include index card quizzes and CLOZE stories (see CLOZE activities in Chapter Seven).

Writing Workshop

Students review target vocabulary words. Students write a composition using as many of the target vocabulary words as possible. Peer editing is encouraged.

In Summary

Pre-reading activities, oral reading strategies, vocabulary building through focused word-study activities, word knowledge assessments and writing workshops help English learners master English language arts standards. English learners need bridging activities to help them master vocabulary as they develop reading comprehension skills. Since English learners cross grade levels, these strategies are important for all teachers.

Targeting Vocabulary Words for English Learners

- Systematic vocabulary instruction using the *Rule of 3*
- Vocabulary: parts of Speech Word Wall
- Use word maps
- Use the "What's My Ending?" technique with vocabulary in sentences taken from the context of the reading selection.
- Writer's Journal: Write a story using new words
- Vocabulary worksheet
- Give students 10 exposures to new vocabulary. This can include in-class exposures as well as homework assignments.
- Word Journals: Students write 10–15 words in their journals every day. Words may be taken from literature, social science, or natural science selections. Homework assignments can include some of the pages in the Activities Section which ask students to create visuals for words as well as written definitions.
- Verb Change: Students underline the verbs in a passage then rewrite the passage using verbs of another tense.

Games to Develop Vocabulary

Context BINGO

This game can be used to develop new vocabulary words across content areas. Have students write the words from the subject-area reading selection on the bingo grid. Ask students to work with a partner. One student reads the definition of a word or gives a synonym for the word in a sentence context. The other student puts a marker on the correct word. The student putting the marker down must also write the word in the sentence context on a whiteboard.

The game can also be played by writing the word definitions on the grid. The student's partner then calls out the word and the paired student must put the marker on the correct definition.

Who Wants to Be a Millionaire?

The teacher gives definitions to words which are tiered from easy (worth $100) to the most difficult (worth $100,000,000). Students need to match definitions to words.

For variation, have students give the definition and use the word in a sentence on a whiteboard.

Synonym Match

Using 3 x 5 cards, write 30–40 words and their synonyms, one word or synonym per card.

Play the game as you would play Concentration. Shuffle the cards and place them face down. Students turn over two cards at a time. They try to match the word with its synonym. Students keep the cards of the pairs they match. The student with the most pairs wins.

Scrabble

Have students make words for Scrabble. In order to get the points for the word, however, the student must write a sentence for each word and read it to the group.

Prefix and Suffix Cargo Ship

Draw a ship on the board. Draw a number of boxes on the ship which contain different prefixes and suffixes. Then give the students a list of words from which to choose. Students unload a prefix or suffix from the cargo boxes on the ship. Students add the prefix or suffix to a word, and then give the meaning of the word with and without the prefix or suffix. This game can be played in pairs by putting it on a worksheet. Students color the squares as they remove the cargo by creating words using prefixes or suffixes. Older students can create their own games using prefixes and suffixes

Picturemania

Write a series of adjectives on cards. Have students illustrate the adjectives on other cards. Line the words up or put them in a pocket chart. Have students find the picture in the stack of cards that matches the word. A variation of this game would be to divide the class into two teams. Team One selects a word. One player on Team Two draws a picture on a whiteboard to illustrate the word, and writes the word on the whiteboard.

After-School Word Search

1. Give students 10 target words for homework.

2. Give students points for reading billboards, posters or newspaper articles.

3 points: Tell the teacher where you heard or saw the target words.

5 points: Bring a newspaper article where the words are used.

10 points: Bring a newspaper article where the words are used and write sentences using the words.

15 points: Find the target words on the Internet and do research online to find the meanings of the words as used in the online context.

Think About Discussion Questions

1. Think about and review the vocabulary development standards for your grade level. Create a content-based activity for the subject you teach integrating one of your grade level vocabulary standards. If you teach multiple subjects, create an activity for a subject area other than language arts.

2. Review the English language development standards for your grade level on your state's Department of Education Web site. Compare and contrast the English language development standards for *Fluency and Systematic Vocabulary Development* to the English language arts vocabulary standards.

Reflection on Teaching Vocabulary Targeting Grade Level Standards

1. Reflect upon the students in your class. Make a quick list of your students. Analyze their performance in the subject you teach. What is the argument that would cause you to conclude that *there is a relationship between student subject area performance and the mastery of vocabulary standards?*

2. Reflect on how you could use the After-School Word Search on page 90 to help students master the content vocabulary in the subject or subjects you teach.

Chapter 7

Vocabulary Building Activities

The Rule of 3

Research shows that student understanding and retention of new vocabulary words can be substantially enhanced by the introduction of entertaining and challenging vocabulary-building activities.

Now that you've learned the powerful *Rule of 3* and the importance of vocabulary development for academic achievement across subject areas, you may be determined to spend 2 ten minute periods a day focused on vocabulary development. If you have made this decision, this section of the book gives you a number of vocabulary development standards-based activities that are sequenced from kindergarten to high school. It is important to note here that students in higher grades may not have mastered lower level vocabulary standards and may need to be taught these standards.

A middle school student may still not have mastered the prefixes and suffixes which are part of the third grade standards. The activities in this section of the book will help this student master prefixes and suffixes.

Many of the activities can also serve as an example for the teacher to create his or her own activities for developing vocabulary words. For example, the *Cloze technique* of filling in words in context is a powerful vocabulary building activity and can be used at any grade level. Categorizing, an important vocabulary standard for kindergarten and first graders, can be practiced with the vocabulary activities in this book, as well as with words from content area textbooks.

Vocabulary activities can be used for small group follow up and homework activities. The charts that ask the students to find a synonym, identify a part of speech, write a sentence and make an illustration are appropriate for grades 2–12. These charts can become part of a student's cumulative vocabulary notebook. Students can refer back to these notebooks when they need vocabulary words for writing assignments.

Charts that require students to use the dictionary or thesaurus are valuable, especially for students from fourth grade through high school. Using the dictionary and thesaurus are important vocabulary development skills. All students should have a dictionary and thesaurus both at school and at home.

How and when you use these activities is up to you. These activities can be used across content areas to develop vocabulary. They are just as powerful with social studies, science and mathematical vocabulary. These activities combined with teaching vocabulary using the *Rule of 3* will prove their worth as valuable learning tools. You will find that as your students learn more vocabulary, their reading comprehension will increase. Teaching vocabulary also helps to close the achievement gap for lower socioeconomic students and English learners.

So now let the powerful teaching of vocabulary begin!

Tier One: Words with concrete referents

table
woman
rock
run

Tier Two: Words critical to the understanding of the content selection and interdisciplinary words.

consequence
organize
inertia
communication

Tier Three: Words tied to the description of nouns and verbs and subject specific words.

respectfully, outrageously

United States

diptheria

Teacher Worksheet 7–1

Reading Selection Vocabulary Worksheet

Level One: Words with concrete referents.

Level Two: Words critical to the understanding of the content selection and interdisciplinary words.

Level Three: Words tied to the description of nouns and verbs and subject specific words.

Example: respectfully, outrageously, United States

Teach vocabulary words using the Rule of 3. Identify 10 words with students and then put the words in the appropriate level. Concentrate on tier 2 interdisciplinary words for vocabulary instruction.

ELD Standard:
Identify the meaning of English words.

ELA Standard:
Use sentence and word context to find the meaning of unknown words.

Grouping Vocabulary Words in 3 Tiers

List vocabulary words in one of the three categories

Tier One: Words with concrete referents.

Tier Two: Words that are critical for the understanding of the story.

Tier Three: Words tied to descriptions of nouns and verbs. Example: *respectfully, outrageously and subject specific words.*

Tier One: Words with concrete referents

Tier Two: Words critical to the understanding of the content selection and interdisciplinary words.

Tier Three: Words tied to the description of nouns and verbs and subject specific words.

1 Vocabulary Definitions	2 Multiple Meaning Words	3 Vocabulary in Context
• A _____ is a kind of • To _____ is to • _____ means • A _____ that is _____ is _____ • A _____ is most like a _____ • Something that is _____ is _____ • Un_____ means not _____ • A _____ is a _____ • To _____ something is to _____ • Someone who has _____, has _____ • A _____ is its _____ • A _____ is the same as _____ • A _____ is someone who _____ • A _____ is like a _____ • Someone who is _____ is _____	A multiple meaning word is a word that has several meanings. The meaning of the underlined multiple meaning word must be determined from the sentence context. Example: *How many **steps** must Maria climb to get to the 10th floor?* In which sentence below does the word **steps** mean the same as in the sentence above? A. He took five steps in the mud. **B. Run up the steps.** C. There are four steps to making cookies. D. She steps lightly on the new grass.	The meaning of the underlined word must be determined from the sentence context. Example: *The ship was carrying only one car, but it was carrying **numerous** bikes.* **Numerous** means: A. funny B. noisy C. silly **D. many**

Teacher Worksheet 7–2

Standardized Testing Format for Types of Vocabulary Questions

This chart lists three ways that standardized achievement tests present vocabulary questions. Note the language, format and structure of each.

ELD Standard:
Use sentence and word context to find the meaning of unknown words.

ELA Standard:
Distinguish and interpret words with multiple meanings.

Standardized Testing Format for
Types of Vocabulary Questions

This chart lists three ways that standardized achievement tests present vocabulary questions. Note the language, format and structure of each.

1 Vocabulary Definitions	2 Multiple Meaning Words	3 Vocabulary in Context

• A _____ is a kind of
 	
• To _____ is to
 	
• _____ means
 	
• A _____ that is
 	
  _____ is _____
 	
• A _____ is most like a
 	
  _____
 	
• Something that is _____ is
 	
  _____
 	
• Un_____ means not
 	
  _____
 	
• A _____ is a
 	
• To _____ something
 	
  is to _____
 	
• Someone who has _____,
 	
  has _____
 	
• A _____ is its
 	
• A _____ is the
 	
  same as _____
 	
• A _____ is someone who
 	
  _____ are _____
 	
• A _____ is like a _____
 	
• Someone who is _____ is
	A multiple meaning word is a word that has several meanings. The meaning of the underlined multiple meaning word must be determined from the sentence context.
	
	Example:
	How many __steps__ must Maria climb to get to the 10th floor?
	
	In which sentence below does the word __steps__ mean the same as in the sentence above?
	
	A. He took five steps in the mud.
	
	B. Run up the steps.
	
	C. There are four steps to making cookies.
	
	D. She steps lightly on the new grass.
		The meaning of the underlined word must be determined from the sentence context.
		
		Example:
		The ship was carrying only one car, but it was carrying __numerous__ bikes.
		
		__Numerous__ means:
		
		A. funny
		
		B. noisy
		
		C. silly
		
		D. many

Lower Elementary Vocabulary Building Activities

Standards-based

Student Vocabulary Building Worktexts with complete grade level critical words for grades one through six are available at younglighteducate.com.

Object	Smooth or Rough
porcupine	
rabbit	
feather	
alligator	
mirror	

Categorization

Discuss each picture with students. Label each item as *smooth* or *rough*.

Ask students the question: "Is this *smooth* or *rough*?"

Have students write the word *smooth* or *rough* next to the object.

Note to the teacher:
Each teacher worksheet is followed by a student worksheet.

ELD Standard:
Ask and answer simple questions.

ELA Standard:
Categorize groups of words.

Smooth or Rough

Name each picture. Label each item as **smooth** or **rough**.

Ask a partner the question: "Is this **smooth** or **rough**?"

Write the word **smooth** or **rough** next to the picture.

Object	**Smooth or Rough**
porcupine	
rabbit	
feather	
alligator	
mirror	

Example:

T-shirt

arm
_____

shirt

_____

glove

_____

zipper

_____

sock

_____

dress

_____

shoe

_____

jacket

_____

coat

_____

Teacher Worksheet 7–4
Categorization

Ask students the question:
What body part(s) can you name for each item?

(*Some items have more than one acceptable body part.*)

Have students identify the body part that the arrows point to.

ELD Standard:
Ask and answer simple questions.

ELA Standard:
Categorize groups of words.

Body Parts

Ask a partner the question: ***What body part(s) can you name for each item?***
Name the body part that the arrows point to.

Example:
T-shirt

arm
_____

shirt
_____

glove
_____

zipper
_____

sock
_____

dress
_____

shoe
_____

jacket
_____

coat
_____

Land	Air	Water

train

sailboat

plane

bicycle

ship

helicopter

Teacher Worksheet 7–5

Categorization

Teach students the concept of categorization. Have students make a mind map of things to wear, places to go, programs to watch on television. Have students categorize ways to travel by *land*, *air* or *water*.

Ask: **How are things that travel in the air alike?**

Ask: **How are things that travel on the ground alike?**

Ask: **How are things that travel in the water alike?**

ELD Standard:
Categorize words.

ELA Standard:
Categorize groups of words.

Travel by Land, Air or Water

Find ways to travel by *land*, by *air*, or on *water*.

Write the words in the correct box.

Tell the ways to travel by land, air, or water to a partner.

Land	Air	Water

train

sailboat

plane

bicycle

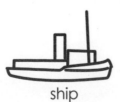

ship

helicopter

Air	Road	Track

Use these vocabulary words.

car	limousine	train
bus	plane	light rail
subway train	jet	helicopter
motorcycle	bicycle	rocket

Teacher Worksheet 7–6
Categorization

Teach the meaning of the vocabulary words using the *Rule of 3*.

Have students categorize words.

Ask: *How are all the types of air transportation alike?*

ELD Standard:
Categorize common words.

ELA Standard:
Categorize groups of words.

Travel

Read the vocabulary words to a partner.

Put the words in the correct box.

Ask: *Does a car drive in the air, on a road or on a track?*
   Does a jet fly in the air, on the road or on a track

Air	Road	Track

Use these vocabulary words.

car	limousine	train
bus	plane	light rail
subway train	jet	helicopter
motorcycle	bicycle	rocket

BINGO for Vocabulary Building

Teach students two ways to play BINGO:

1. Write vocabulary words in the boxes and play BINGO.

2. Write definitions of words in the boxes. Have students tell you the word before putting a marker in the box.

ELD Standard:
Identify common English words and definitions.

ELA Standard:
Match words with definitions.

BINGO for Vocabulary Building

Here are two ways to play BINGO with a partner:

1. Write vocabulary words in the boxes and play BINGO.
2. Write definitions of words in the boxes. Have a partner tell you the word before putting a marker in the box.

Use these vocabulary words.

three	pre-assembled	moved
haul	rented	one	garden

1. Mobile homes can be _____ to another place.

2. Mobile homes are _____ at a factory.

3. A truck can _____ a mobile home away.

4. The lot a mobile home is placed on is _____.

5. The mobile home has _____ bedrooms.

6. The mobile home has _____ dining room.

7. The mobile home has a small _____ of roses.

Teacher Worksheet 7–8

Identify Words in Context

Teach the meaning of the vocabulary words using the **Rule of 3**.

Teach students to use the context to figure out the correct word to use in each sentence.

Have students read the sentences to a partner to determine if the word makes sense in the sentence.

ELD Standard:
Use context clues.

ELA Standard:
Use sentence and word context to find the meaning of unknown words.

Identify Words in Context

Identify the vocabulary words.

Write in the correct word in each sentence.

Read the sentences to a partner.

three   pre-assembled   moved   haul   rented   one   garden

1. Mobile homes can be _____ to another place.

2. Mobile homes are _____ at a factory.

3. A truck can _____ a mobile home away.

4. The lot a mobile home is placed on is _____.

5. The mobile home has _____ bedrooms.

6. The mobile home has _____ dining room.

7. The mobile home has a small _____ of roses.

Vocabulary Words: bread, dough, mixing, making, the

The baker is _____

_____

The baker is _____

_____

Vocabulary Words: carrying groceries, wearing, walking

The man is _____

_____

The woman is _____ glasses.

The woman is _____ next to the man.

Vocabulary Words: fence, climbing, helping, over

The boys are _____ over the _____

One boy is _____ the other boy get _____ the fence.

ELD Standard:
Use context clues.

ELA Standard:
Use sentence and word context to complete the sentence.

Finish the Sentences

Use the vocabulary words to finish the sentences based on what you see in the pictures.

Vocabulary Words: bread, dough, mixing, the, making,

The baker is _____

_____

The baker is _____

_____

Vocabulary Words: carrying groceries, wearing, walking

The man is _____

_____

The lady is_____ glasses.

The lady is_____ next to the man.

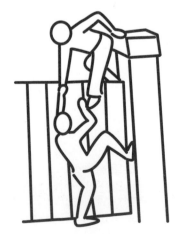

Vocabulary Words: fence, climbing, helping, over

The boys are _____ over

the _____

One boy is _____ the other

boy get _____ the fence.

Use these vocabulary words.

rake leaves   basket   tree   falling   trash

_____

_____

_____

_____

_____

_____

_____

_____

_____

_____

_____

_____

_____

_____

_____

Teacher Worksheet 7–10
Narrative Writing

Have students write a story about the pictures using the vocabulary words given.

Have students use the writing checklist.

Have students read their stories to a partner.

ELD Standard:
Write a short narrative.

ELA Standard:
Write a narrative.

Narrative Writing

Write a story about the pictures using the vocabulary words given.

Use the writing checklist.

Read your story to a partner.

Use these vocabulary words.

rake leaves   basket   tree   falling   trash

_____

_____

_____

_____

_____

_____

_____

_____

_____

_____

_____

_____

Spelling Friends cl_, bl_, gl_, fl_

cloud	blow	glove	flower
climate	blame	glow	flip
clock	blink	glitter	flute
climb	blimp	glue	flew
clown	block	glide	flight

Word	N / V*	Sentence
climate		
cloud		
blow		
blame		
glide		
glove		
flower		
flew		
flight		

* **N** for **Noun**
   V for **Verb**

Teacher Worksheet 7–11
Consonant Blends

● Have students blend the words on the Spelling Friends Chart.

● Discuss the meaning of each word. Use each word in a sentence.

● Have students label each word as a **noun** or a **verb**.

Next:

● Have students read the words on the bottom chart.

● Complete the chart.

● Label each word with **N** for **noun** or **V** for **verb**.

● Have students read the sentences to a partner.

ELD Standard:
Identify consonant blends.

ELA Standard:
Generate the sounds from all the letters and letter patterns including consonant blends.

Consonant Blends

Read the Spelling Friends Chart. Discuss the meaning of each word.

Use each word in a sentence. Label each word as a **noun** or a **verb**.

Next:

Read the words on the chart. Complete the chart with a partner.

Label each word with a **N for noun** or **V for verb**. Read the sentences to a partner.

Spelling Friends cl_, bl_, gl_, fl_			
cloud	blow	glove	flower
climate	blame	glow	flip
clock	blink	glitter	flute
climb	blimp	glue	flew
clown	block	glide	flight

Word	N / V*	Sentence
climate		
cloud		
blow		
blame		
glide		
glove		
flower		
flew		
flight		

* **N** for **Noun**
  V for **Verb**

Spelling Friends

_or_	_oy_	_oo_
more	boy	moon
tore	Roy	soon
bore	joy	spoon
core	soy	balloon
chore	annoy	bloom
shore	enjoy	cartoon
store	toy	noon

Word	N / V*	Sentence
tore		
store		
chore		
boy		
enjoy		
toy		
spoon		
balloon		
cartoon		

* **N** for **Noun**
V for **Verb**

Teacher Worksheet 7–12
Word Families

Teach the spelling patterns on the top chart.

Discuss the meaning of the words.

Have students read the bottom chart.

Have students complete the chart and read their sentences to a partner.

ELD Standard:
Identify word families.

ELA Standard:
Read common word families.

Name_____ Date _____

Word Families

● Read the words with the spelling friends _or_, _oy and _oo_.
● Read the words in the bottom chart.
● Complete the chart. Read your sentences to a partner.

Spelling Friends		
_or_	_oy	_oo_
more	boy	moon
tore	Roy	soon
bore	joy	spoon
core	soy	balloon
chore	annoy	bloom
shore	enjoy	cartoon
store	toy	noon

Word	N / V*	Sentence
tore		
store		
chore		
boy		
enjoy		
toy		
spoon		
balloon		
cartoon		

* **N** for **Noun**
  V for **Verb**

Nouns	Verbs	Adjectives

Teacher Worksheet 7–13

Parts of Speech: The Word Wall

Create a **Word Wall** using the parts of speech.

Color-code the parts of speech:

- Use *blue* 3 X 5 index cards for *nouns*.
- Use *yellow* 3 X 5 index cards for *verbs*.
- Use *pink* 3 X 5 index cards for *adjectives*.

Make index cards for the reading selection.

Have students put the words on the **Word Wall** under the correct parts of speech and write the words in alphabetical order on the chart.

ELD Standard:
Identify parts of speech.

ELA Standard:
Identify and correctly use various parts of speech.

Name_____ Date _____

Parts of Speech: The Word Wall

Create a **Word Wall** using the parts of speech.

Color-code the parts of speech of the vocabulary words in the reading selection:

- Use *blue* 3 X 5 index cards for nouns.
- Use *yellow* 3 X 5 index cards for verbs.
- Use *pink* 3 X 5 index cards for adjectives.

Write the words on the chart under the correct parts of speech. Put the words under each part of speech in alphabetical order.

Nouns	*Verbs*	*Adjectives*

Upper Elementary Vocabulary Building Activities

Standards-based

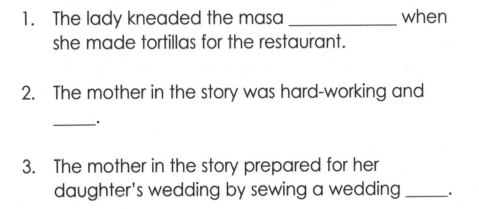

Use these vocabulary words.

wrote	whiteboard	game	tickets
players	drove	school	caring
vigorously	tenth	dress	food
lives	team	world	live
refrigerator	train		

1. The lady kneaded the masa _____ when she made tortillas for the restaurant.

2. The mother in the story was hard-working and ____.

3. The mother in the story prepared for her daughter's wedding by sewing a wedding ____.

4. The teacher ____ the problem on the ____.

5. Where in the ____ does he ____?

6. The elevator went to the ____ floor of the apartment building.

7. Is there any ____ in the ____?

8. Marcos ____ the car to the elementary ____.

9. The conductor took the ____ on the ____.

10. The tiger ____ in the jungle.

11. All the ____ on the ____ played in the baseball ____.

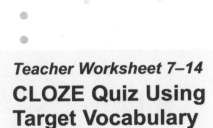

Teacher Worksheet 7–14

CLOZE Quiz Using Target Vocabulary

Have students write the numbers 1 through 11 on a sheet of paper.

Read the sentences.

Have students write the missing word or words in each sentence. Have students write the definitions of the words on another sheet of paper.

ELD Standard:
Use context clues.

ELA Standard:
Use sentence and word context to find the meaning of unknown words.

CLOZE Quiz Using Target Vocabulary

● Read the sentences below.
● Write the missing word or words in each sentence.
● Write the definitions for the words on another sheet of paper.

Use these vocabulary words.

wrote	whiteboard	game	tickets	players	drove
school	caring	vigorously	tenth	dress	food
lives	team	world	live	refrigerator	train

1. The lady kneaded the masa _____ when she made tortillas for the restaurant.

2. The mother in the story was hard-working and _____.

3. The mother in the story prepared for her daughter's wedding by sewing a wedding _____.

4. The teacher _____ the problem on the _____.

5. Where in the _____ does he _____?

6. The elevator went to the _____ floor of the apartment building.

7. Is there any _____ in the _____?

8. Marcos _____ drove the car to the elementary _____.

9. The conductor took the _____ on the _____.

10. The tiger _____ in the jungle.

11. All the _____ on the _____ played in the baseball _____.

Singular Nouns	Plural	Examples
Nouns ending with:		
s	Add -es	bus = buses
ss	Add -es	class = classes glass = glasses
x	Add -es	box = boxes
z (or z sound)	Add -es	rose = roses
ch	Add -es	match = matches watch = watches sandwich = sandwiches
sh	Add -es	bush = bushes wish = wishes dish = dishes

Create Plurals

Use the chart to teach the rules for creating plurals by adding **-es** to nouns that end with **s**, **ss**, **x**, **z**, **ch** and **sh,** using the chart.

Brainstorm other words that end in **s**, **ss**, **x**, **z**, **ch**, and **sh**.

These are _____.   These are _____.

These are _____.   These are _____.

These are _____.   These are _____.

These are _____.   These are _____.

ELD Standard:
Create plurals.

ELA Standard:
Identify and use singular and plural nouns.

Name_____ Date _____

Create Plurals

Add **-es** to nouns that end with **s**, **ss**, **x**, **z**, **ch**, and **sh** to create the plural.

Write the correct plural noun in the sentence under each picture. Read the sentences to a partner.

Singular Nouns	Plural	Examples
Nouns ending with:		
s	**Add -es**	bus = buses
ss	**Add -es**	class = classes glass = glasses
x	**Add -es**	box = boxes
z (or z sound)	**Add -es**	rose = roses
ch	**Add -es**	match = matches watch = watches sandwich = sandwiches
sh	**Add -es**	bush = bushes wish = wishes dish = dishes

These are _____.

These are _____.

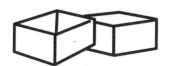

These are _____.

These are _____.

These are _____.

These are _____.

These are _____.

These are _____.

Travel		
Reasons for Travel	**Kinds of Places**	**Kinds of Activities**
Why are you traveling?	Where are you going?	What are you going to do?
Why are you traveling?	Where are you going?	What are you going to do?
Why are you traveling?	Where are you going?	What are you going to do?

Teacher Worksheet 7–16

Identify Concepts with the Concept Chart

Have students categorize different travel experiences. Have students list the reasons for travel, where they are going and the kinds of activities they have planned with their families.

Have students ask and answer these questions with a partner and fill out the chart:

"Why are you traveling?" (reasons)

"Where are you going?" (locations, destinations)

"What are you going to do?" (types of activities)

ELD Standard:
Ask and answer simple questions.

ELA Standard:
Categorize groups of words.

Name_____ Date _____

Identify Concepts with the Concept Chart

Categorize different types of travel.

List the reasons for the travel, the places of destination and the types of activities planned.

Ask and answer these questions with a partner and fill out the chart:

● *"Why are you traveling?"* (reasons)

● *"Where are you going?"* (kinds of places)

● *"What are you going to do?"* (kinds of activities planned)

Travel		
Reasons for Travel	**Kinds of Places**	**Kinds of Activities**
Why are you traveling?	Where are you going?	What are you going to do?
Why are you traveling?	Where are you going?	What are you going to do?
Why are you traveling?	Where are you going?	What are you going to do?

Word	Picture or Drawing

Teacher Worksheet 7–17

My Picture Dictionary

This worksheet personalizes the meaning of words. Students list five new vocabulary words from a content selection. Students draw a picture to illustrate each word and explain their illustrations to a partner.

ELD Standard:
Write common words.

ELA Standard:
Match words to pictures.

Name_____ Date _____

My Picture Dictionary

Write five new vocabulary words.

Draw a picture for each word. Describe your pictures to a partner.

Word	Picture or Drawing

Word	Picture	Sentence

Teacher Worksheet 7–18

Identify Word Meanings

Teach students new content words using the *Rule of 3*.

Have students illustrate each word and use it in a sentence.

Have students describe their pictures and read their sentences to a partner.

ELD Standard:
Match words to pictures.

ELA Standard:
Write a simple sentence.

Identify Word Meanings

Draw a picture and write a sentence for each word.

Describe the pictures to a partner.

Read the sentences to a partner.

Word	Picture	Sentence

1. A <u>boulder</u> is a kind of . . .
   ○ crayon
   ○ pencil
   ○ rock
   ○ flower

   _____

2. <u>Multicolored</u> means . . .
   ○ many colors
   ○ one color
   ○ big
   ○ mean

   _____

3. <u>Next to</u> means . . .
   ○ in front of
   ○ under
   ○ beside
   ○ over

   _____

4. Something that is <u>polished</u> is . . .
   ○ old
   ○ yellow
   ○ rough
   ○ shiny

   _____

5. A <u>pebble</u> is a . . .
   ○ large rock
   ○ pineapple
   ○ shoe
   ○ small rock

   _____

Teacher Worksheet 7–19

Identify Word Meanings

Read each phrase with students.

Discuss the meaning of each word.

Have students fill in the bubble for the correct answer.

Have students draw a picture for each <u>underlined</u> vocabulary word and write the word under the picture.

ELD Standard:
Identify meaning of English words.

ELA Standard:
Demonstrate knowledge of specificity of grade-level words.

Name_____ Date _____

Identify Word Meaning

Read each phrase and fill in the bubble for each correct answer.

Draw a picture for each underlined vocabulary word. Write the word under the picture.

1. A <u>boulder</u> is a kind of . . .
   - ◯ crayon
   - ◯ pencil
   - ◯ rock
   - ◯ flower

   _____

2. <u>Multicolored</u> means . . .
   - ◯ many colors
   - ◯ one color
   - ◯ big
   - ◯ mean

   _____

3. <u>Next to</u> means . . .
   - ◯ in front of
   - ◯ under
   - ◯ beside
   - ◯ over

   _____

4. Something that is <u>polished</u> is . . .
   - ◯ old
   - ◯ yellow
   - ◯ rough
   - ◯ shiny

   _____

5. A <u>pebble</u> is a . . .
   - ◯ large rock
   - ◯ pineapple
   - ◯ shoe
   - ◯ small rock

   _____

Word	N/A*	Picture	Sentence
rough			
soft			
smooth			
multicolored			
rabbit			
boulder			
pebble			
feather			

* **A** for **Adjective**
  N for **Noun**

Teacher Worksheet 7–20

Identify Parts of Speech

Teach the parts of speech — *adjectives* and *nouns*.

> *adjective: defines or describes a noun*

> *noun: a name of a person, place or thing*

Have students label each word with **A** for *adjective* or **N** for *noun*.

Have students draw a picture and write a sentence for each word.

Have students describe the pictures and read the sentences to a partner.

ELD Standard:
Identify parts of speech.

ELA Standard:
Identify and use various parts of speech.

Name_____ Date _____

Identify Word Meaning

Identify the parts of speech—*adjectives* and *nouns*.

   adjective: defines or describes a noun   noun: is the name of a person, place or thing

Label each word with **A** for *adjective* or **N** for *noun*.

Draw a picture and write a sentence for each word.

Describe the pictures and read the sentences to a partner.

Word	Noun or Adjective	Picture	Sentence

Word	Part of Speech	Sentence from Context	Picture

Teacher Worksheet 7–21

Parts of Speech Vocabulary Chart

Daily Core Vocabulary Development Sheet

Teach students to use the
Rule of 3:

1. Spell and say the word to a partner. One student dictates; the other student writes the word. Switch roles. Write the part of speech for each word.

2. Find the word in the reading selection in context. Write the sentence.

3. Draw a picture to illustrate the word in the sentence.

ELD Standard:
Identify parts of speech.

ELA Standard:
Identify and use parts of speech.

Name_____ Date _____

Parts of Speech Vocabulary Chart

1. Spell and say the words to a partner. One student dictates, the other student writes the word. Switch roles. Write the part of speech for each word.

2. Find the word in the reading selection in context. Write the sentence.

3. Draw a picture to illustrate the word in the sentence.

Word	Part of Speech	Sentence from Context	Picture

Yesterday	Today
helped	help
walked	walk
talked	talk
played	play
watched	watch
answered	answer
joined	join

1. What did Maria do yesterday?
   She _____ her father rake the leaves.

2. What did Pao do yesterday?
   He _____ to the park after school and
   played basketball.

3. What did Mike do yesterday?
   He _____ on the phone for hours.

4. What did he do yesterday?
   He _____ video games at the
   community center.

5. What did she do yesterday?
   She _____ the sun rise over the desert.

6. What did he do yesterday?
   He _____ the cell phone.

7. What did she do yesterday?
   She _____ the swim club.

Teacher Worksheet 7–22

Use Past Tense Verbs

Teach students that you add **-ed** to create the past tense.

Ask students:
What did you do yesterday?
What are you doing today?

Write student's answers on the board underlining the past tense verbs.

List regular verbs on the board and then have students add an **ed** to create the past tense.

Have students use each past tense verb in a sentence.

ELD Standard:
Identify parts of speech.

ELA Standard:
Identify and use past, present and future verb tenses properly.

Use Past Tense Verbs

Add **-ed** to create the past tense. Read the words on the chart to a partner.

Ask a partner: **What did you do yesterday? What are you doing today?**

Write the correct past tense verb in each sentence. Ask and answer the questions with a partner.

Yesterday	Today
helped	help
walked	walk
talked	talk
played	play
watched	watch
answered	answer
joined	join

1. What did Maria do yesterday?

   She _____ her father rake the leaves.

2. What did Pao do yesterday?

   He _____ to the park after school and played basketball.

3. What did Mike do yesterday?

   He _____ on the phone for hours.

4. What did he do yesterday?

   He _____ video games at the community center.

5. What did she do yesterday?

   She _____ the sun rise over the desert.

6. What did he do yesterday?

   He _____ the cell phone.

7. What did she do yesterday?

   She _____ the swim club.

Irregular Verbs

A verb is an action word.
It tells what someone or something does.

A verb in the present tense tells what is happening now.
The boy plays with the ball.

A verb in the past tense tells what happened in the past.
Yesterday, the boy played with the ball.

You add <u>ed</u> to verbs to make them past tense.
play = played

You add <u>d</u> if the verbs end in <u>e</u>.
like = liked

You double the final consonant to verbs that end with one vowel and one consonant.
hop = hopped
stir = stirred

You must learn these irregular past tense verbs.

Verb	Past	Past (has, have, had)
come	came	*has, have, had* come
teach	taught	*has, have, had* taught
drive	drove	*has, have, had* driven
eat	ate	*has, have, had* eaten
give	gave	*has, have, had* given
go	went	*has, have, had* gone
ride	rode	*has, have, had* ridden
see	saw	*has, have, had* seen
write	wrote	*has, have, had* written
am, is, are	was, were	*has, have, had* been

Teacher Worksheet 7–23
Irregular Past Tense Verbs

Teach students irregular verbs:

● You do not always end in *-ed* to form the past tense of verbs.

● Verbs that do not end in *-ed* are called irregular verbs. You must learn these irregular verbs.

Have students use each of these verbs in a sentence.

ELD Standard:
Identify parts of speech.

ELA Standard:
Identify and use past, present, and future verb tenses properly.

Irregular Past Tense Verbs

● You do not always add **-ed** to form the past tense of verbs.

● Verbs that do not end in **-ed** are called irregular verbs. You must learn these irregular verbs.

● Use each of the verbs below in a sentence on a separate sheet of paper.

A verb is an action word. It tells what someone or something does.

A verb in the present tense tells what is happening now.
> *The boy plays with the ball.*

A verb in the past tense tells what happened in the past.
> *Yesterday, the boy played with the ball.*

You add **-ed** to verbs to make them past tense.
> *play = played*

You add **-d** if the verbs end in e.
> *like = liked*

You double the final consonant to verbs that end with one vowel and one consonant.
> *hop = hopped*
> *stir = stirred*

You must learn these irregular past tense verbs.

Verb	Past	Past Participle (has, have, had)
come	came	*has, have, had* come
teach	taught	has, have, had taught
drive	drove	has, have, had driven
eat	ate	has, have, had eaten
give	gave	has, have, had given
go	went	has, have, had gone
ride	rode	has, have, had ridden
see	saw	has, have, had seen
write	wrote	has, have, had written
am, is, are	was, were	has, have, had been

Verb	Past	Past Participle (has, have, had)
bring	brought	has, have, had brought
do	did	has, have, had done
draw	drew	has, have, had drawn
fly	flew	has, have, had flown
grow	grew	has, have, had grown
make	made	has, have, had made
sing	sang	has, have, had sung
swim	swam	has, have, had swum
take	took	has, have, had taken
throw	threw	has, have, had thrown

Write a sentence using each past tense verb.
Use a separate piece of paper if you need to.

_____

_____

_____

_____

_____

_____

_____

_____

_____

_____

Irregular Verbs

● Read the irregular past tense verbs on the chart to a partner.

● You do not always add **-ed** to form the past tense of verbs.

● Verbs that do not end in **-ed** are called irregular verbs.

● You must learn these irregular verbs.

Verb	*Past*	*Past Participle* (has, have, had)
bring	brought	has, have, had brought
do	did	has, have, had done
draw	drew	has, have, had drawn
fly	flew	has, have, had flown
grow	grew	has, have, had grown
make	made	has, have, had made
sing	sang	has, have, had sung
swim	swam	has, have, had swum
take	took	has, have, had taken
throw	threw	has, have, had thrown

Write a sentence using each past tense verb.
Use a separate piece of paper if you need to. Read your sentences to a partner.

_____

_____

_____

_____

_____

_____

_____

_____

- You can form the past tense of most verbs by adding the letters **-ed** or **-d** to the verb.

- Verbs that do not end in **-ed** or **-d** to form the past tense are called irregular verbs.

Verb	Past	Past Participle (with has, have, or had)
draw	drew	has, have, had drawn
write	wrote	has, have, had written
do	did	has, have, had done
bring	brought	has, have, had brought
make	made	has, have, had made
take	took	has, have, had taken
throw	threw	has, have, had thrown
grow	grew	has, have, had grown
fly	flew	has, have, had flown

1. In the past, the pilot (fly) _____ a plane with propellers.

2. The baseball player (throw) _____ the ball to first base.

3. The cactus (grow) _____ in the Mojave Desert.

4. The gentleman (bring) _____ the flowers to the party.

5. The cook (make) _____ a seven course dinner.

6. The fir tree (grow) _____ in the north.

7. The artist (draw) _____ the outline of the cathedral.

8. Who (take) _____ the last ice cream cone?

9. Where (do) _____ he go on vacation last year?

Teacher Worksheet 7–25

Irregular Past Tense Verbs in Sentences

Teach irregular past tense verbs and past participles.

Read the words on the chart with students.

Discuss the meaning of each word.

Explain to students that irregular verbs do not follow the rules for creating the past tense.

ELD Standard:
Identify parts of speech.

ELA Standard:
Identify and use past, present, and future verb tenses properly.

Irregular Past Tense Verbs in Sentences

✓ You can form the past tense of most verbs by adding the letters **-ed** or **-d** to the verb.

✓ Verbs that do not end in **-ed** or **-d** to form the past tense are called irregular verbs.

Write the correct past tense form of the verb in parentheses in each sentence.

Read the sentences to a partner.

Verb	Past	Past Participle (has, have, had)
draw	drew	has, have, had drawn
write	wrote	has, have, had written
do	did	has, have, had done
bring	brought	has, have, had brought
make	made	has, have, had made
take	took	has, have, had taken
throw	threw	has, have, had thrown
grow	grew	has, have, had grown
fly	flew	has, have, had flown

1. In the past, the pilot (fly) _____ a plane with propellers.

2. The baseball player (throw) _____ the ball to first base.

3. The cactus (grow) _____ in the Mohave Desert.

4. The gentleman (bring) _____ the flowers to the party.

5. The cook (make) _____ a seven course dinner.

6. The fir tree (grow) _____ in the north.

7. The artist (draw) _____ the outline of the cathedral.

8. Who (take) _____ the last ice cream cone?

9. Where (do) _____ he go on vacation last year?

Imagination Vocabulary Building
imaginary, nonexistent, travel, destination, unicorn, straight, forehead, beautiful, visited, speed, snack, planet

Have you ever had an imaginary friend, someone that only you can hear and see? Every night I travel to a new destination with my imaginary friend. We travel on a unicorn which is an imaginary animal that looks like a horse with a long straight horn on its forehead. The imaginary unicorn is white and has beautiful white wings. My imaginary friend and I jump on the unicorn and fly across the sky at the speed of light. We visit other imaginary planets and find imaginary friends. Last night we visited the imaginary planet of Zentex.

We had an imaginary snack and then played on an imaginary playground. Our imaginary friends were sad to see us go, but it was time to take our imaginary flight back to planet Earth.

Create your own story.

_____

_____

_____

_____

_____

_____

_____

Worksheet 7–26

Imagination Vocabulary Building

Discuss the meaning of the words *imaginary* and *imagination* with students.

Introduce the vocabulary words using the Rule of 3.

Have students read the story to a partner. The partner closes his or her eyes and imagines what is happening in the story. Have students underline the vocabulary words in the story and try to figure out the meaning of the words from context. Have students use the vocabulary words to create an imaginary story with a partner.

ELD Standard:
Use word meanings in context.

ELA Standard:
Use word meanings within an appropriate context.

Imagination Vocabulary Building

● Read the story to a partner. The partner closes his or her eyes and imagines what is happening in the story.

● Underline these vocabulary words in the story: imaginary, travel, destination, unicorn, straight, forehead, beautiful, visited, speed, snack, planet.

● Create your own imaginary story with a partner using the vocabulary words.

Have you ever had an imaginary friend, someone that only you can hear and see? Every night I travel to a new destination with my imaginary friend. We travel on a unicorn which is an imaginary animal that looks like a horse with a long straight horn on its forehead. The imaginary unicorn is white and has beautiful white wings. My imaginary friend and I jump on the unicorn and fly across the sky at the speed of light. We visit other imaginary planets and find imaginary friends. Last night we visited the imaginary planet of Zentex.

We had an imaginary snack and then played on an imaginary playground. Our imaginary friends were sad to see us go, but it was time to take our imaginary flight back to planet Earth.

Create your own story.

_____

_____

_____

_____

_____

_____

_____

_____

_____

Prefix	Meaning	Prefix with Word
un-	means *not*	unclean (not clean)
un-	means *not*	unhappy (not happy)
un-	means *not*	unable (not able)
un-	means *not*	untied (not tied)
un-	means *not*	unreal (not real)
un-	means *not*	unlocked (not locked)

	Word with Prefix	Sentence
not clean	unclean	
not happy		
not able		
not tied		
not real		
not locked		

Teacher Worksheet 7–27
Identify the Prefix *un-*

Identify the simple prefix *un-*.

Tell students the meaning of the prefix *un-* is *not*.

Ask: *What does it mean when I say my shoes are untied?*

Exercise:

Have students say the following words:

> *unclean, unhappy, unable, untie, unreal, unlocked.*

Clap out the syllables.

Write each word using the prefix *un-*. Have students use each word in a sentence.

Discuss the meanings of the words and complete the chart.

ELD Standard:
Identify prefixes and suffixes.

ELA Standard:
Use knowledge of prefixes and suffixes to determine the meaning of words.

Identify the Prefix *un-*

Identify the simple prefix **un-**. Identify the meaning of the prefix **un-** and the words on the chart. Read the words to a partner.

Prefix	Meaning	Prefix with Word
un-	means **not**	unclean (not clean)
un-	means **not**	unhappy (not happy)
un-	means **not**	unable (not able)
un-	means **not**	untied (not tied)
un-	means **not**	unreal (not real)
un-	means **not**	unlocked (not locked)

Exercise:

Say the following words: untied, unhappy, unable, unreal, unlocked, unopened.

Clap out the syllables. Write each word using the prefix **un-**. Use each word in a sentence.

Word	Prefix	Word with Prefix	Word Meaning	Sentence
tied	*un-*	untied	not tied	His shoe laces are untied
happy				
able				
real				
locked				
opened				

Prefix	Meaning	Prefix with Word
re-	means **do it again**	replay (play again)
re-	means **do it again**	rework (work again)
re-	means **do it again**	repaint (paint again)
re-	means **do it again**	redo (do again)
re-	means **do it again**	reclean (clean again)
re-	means **do it again**	reupholster (upholster again)

	Word with Prefix	Sentence
play again	replay	
work again		
paint again		
do again		
clean again		
upholster again		

Identify the Prefix *re-*

Teach the simple prefix *re-*.

The meaning of the prefix *re-* is **to do again**.

Exercise:

Say the following words:

replay, repaint, redo, reclean, reupholster.

Ask: *What does it mean to repaint a room? What does it mean to replay a CD? Why do people reupholster their furniture?*

ELD Standard:
Identify prefixes and suffixes.

ELA Standard:
Use knowledge of prefixes and suffixes to determine the meaning of words.

Identify the Prefix *re-*

Identify the meaning of the prefix **re**-. Identify the meaning of the words with the **re**- prefix.

Read the words on the chart to a partner.

Prefix	Meaning	Prefix with Word
re-	means do it again	replay (play again)
re-	means do it again	rework (work again)
re-	means do it again	repaint (paint again)
re-	means do it again	redo (do again)
re-	means do it again	reattach (attach again)
re-	means do it again	reupholster (unpholster again)

Exercise:

Say the following words: *replay, repaint, redo, reclean, reupholster.*

Write the word with the prefix on the chart and use each word in a sentence.
Read the sentences to a partner.

Word	Prefix	Word with Prefix	Word meaning	Sentence
play	*re-*	replay	play again	She is going to replay the DVD.
work				
paint				
do				
attach				
upholster				

Grade	Base Word	Prefix/Suffix	Meaning	New Word
Two	lock	_un-_	not	unlock
	plant	_re-_	again	replant
	thank	_-ful_	full of	thankful
	home	_-less_	without	homeless
	work	_-er_	one who does	worker
	slow	_-ly_	in a way that is	slowly
	enjoy	_-ment_	act of	enjoyment
	member	_-ship_	state of	membership
	stick	_-y_	like, or full of	sticky

Additional examples: agreement, banker, builder, careful, careless, colorful, deeply, dusty, endless, fearful, friendly, friendship, healthy, hopeful, hopeless, leadership, membership, mighty, movement, painful, painless, quietly, rebuild, refill, remake, rename, reopen, repay, replay, rerun, retell, rewrite, singer, slowly, softly, stormy, successful, unable, uncertain, uneven, unfriendly, unhappy, unhealthy, unkind, unwise

Grade	Base Word	Prefix/Suffix	Meaning	New Word
Three	appear	_dis-_	not, opposite	disappear
	proper	_im-_	not	improper
	stop	_non-_	no	nonstop
	tool	_re-_	again	retool
	fair	_un-_	not, opposite	unfair
	teach	_-er_	one who does	teacher
	hope	_-ful_	full of	hopeful
	fear	_-less_	without	fearless
	quick	_-ly_	in a way that is	quickly
	month	_-ly_	every	monthly
	rust	_-y_	like, full of	rusty
	entertain	_-ment_	state of, act of	entertainment
	member	_-ship_	state of	membership
	happy	_-ness_	state of	happiness

Additional examples: badly, banker, brightness, colorful, dancer, darkness, disconnect, dishonest, dislike, displease, employment, farmer, fearful, friendly, friendship, goodness, healthy, hopeful, illness, immovable, impatient, imperfect, impossible, loudly, lucky, movement, muddy, nonfat, nonfiction, nonstick, painless, painter, powerless, quickly, rebuild, refill, reopen, sickness, softly, stormy, suddenly, unable, unfriendly, unwelcome, wealthy

Grade	Base Word	Prefix/Suffix	Meaning	New Word
Four	atlantic	_trans-_	across	transatlantic
	happy	_un-_	not, opposite	unhappy
	order	_dis-_	not, opposite	disorder
	hope	_-ful_	full of	hopeful
	wait	_-er_	one who does	waiter
	reason	_-able_	able to be	reasonable
	comfort	_-ably_	in a way that is	comfortably
	flex	_-ible_	able to be	flexible
	flex	_-ibly_	in a way that is	flexibly
	connect	_-ion_	act of, state of being	connection

Teacher Worksheet 7–29

List of Prefixes and Suffixes

Teach the list of prefixes and suffixes that are appropriate to the students' grade levels.

ELD Standard:
Identify prefixes and suffixes.

ELA Standard:
Know common roots, affixes, and suffixes.

Name_____ **Date** _____

Prefixes

● Read the prefixes and new words.

● Fill in the correct word in each sentence.

● Read the sentences to a partner.

Prefix	Meaning	New Word
re-	**again**	retell
un-	**not**	untied
dis-	**not**	disagree
bi-	**two**	biannually
im-	**not**	improper
tri-	**three**	tricycle
mis-	**not**	mismanage
pre-	**before**	preschool
pre-	**before**	preplanned
dis-	**not**	distrust

1. The couple _____ on how much they should spend for a new vehicle.

2. The boy was four years old. He was attending a local _____.

3. The report on the company's earning was issued _____.

4. It is _____ behavior not to thank someone for a present.

5. The clown was riding on a _____, which is a bike with three wheels.

6. Maria wanted to _____ the cheerful story over and over again.

7. Don't _____ the way you spend your monthly earnings.

8. His multicolored shoe laces were _____ when he left for school.

9. Do you _____ him because he never tells the truth?

10. The birthday party was _____. The guests were invited a month in advance.

Interdisciplinary Vocabulary Development: The Rule of 3

Vocabulary Words: counter, goldfish, bowl, swim, continue, splatter, clean, put

1. What did you do when your goldfish bowl fell off the kitchen counter?

_____

_____

_____

_____

_____

Vocabulary Words: bowl, replace, buy, pet store, shop, put, water

2. How did you get a new goldfish bowl to replace the broken bowl?
   Where did you buy another goldfish?

_____

_____

_____

_____

_____

Teacher Worksheet 7–30

Vocabulary, Consequence and Sequel

Explain consequences by reviewing simple practice examples.

What happens if you drop a glass bottle of milk?

Discuss the sequence of events:

- You must clean up the mess.
- You might have to bandage your hand.
- You need to buy a new bottle of milk.

Have students write the sequence of events for numbers 1 and 2 using the vocabulary words listed.

ELD Standard:
Identify sequence of events.

ELA Standard:
Recognize cause and effect relationships.

Vocabulary, Consequence and Sequel

What happens if you drop a glass bottle of milk?

What is the sequence of events?

1. You must clean up the mess.

2. You might have to bandage your hand.

3. You need to buy a new bottle of milk.

Answer each question. Tell what you did.

Use the vocabulary words to write a sequence of events.

Vocabulary Words: counter, goldfish, bowl, swim, continue, splatter, clean, put

1. What did you do when your goldfish bowl fell of the kitchen counter?

    Answer the question. Use the vocabulary words to write a sequence of events.

_____

_____

_____

_____

_____

Vocabulary Words: bowl, replace, buy, pet store, shop, put, water

2. How did you get a new bowl to replace the broken bowl?
   Where did you buy another goldfish?

    Answer the question. Use the vocabulary words to write a sequence of events.

_____

_____

_____

_____

_____

1. **The sun gives us _light_.**

   In which sentence does the word light mean the same thing as in the sentence above?
   - ○ The suitcase was very light.
   - ● The light from the lamp is too bright.
   - ○ Please wear a light jacket.
   - ○ The matches won't light.

2. **That tomato is still _green_.**

   In which sentence does the word green mean the same thing as in the sentence above?
   - ○ She hit the golf ball on the green.
   - ○ I have a green coat.
   - ● The plum is so green that I can't eat it.
   - ○ The clerk was too green to know how to do the job.

Teacher Worksheet 7–31

Multiple Meaning Words

Teach multiple meaning words. Tell students that some words in English have more than one meaning. Discuss the multiple meanings of the italicized words.

3. **Write a _note_ to the scientist.**

   In which sentence does the word note mean the same thing as in the sentence above?.
   - ● I read the note aloud.
   - ○ Be sure you note the directions.
   - ○ He played a low note on the piano.
   - ○ When she sang, she reached a high note.

4. **The first _batter_ hit a home run.**

   In which sentence does the word batter mean the same thing as in the sentence above?.
   - ○ Please mix the cake batter.
   - ○ A boat that is not tied well will batter the dock.
   - ○ Is that the batter for the cookies?
   - ● Who will be the next batter up to bat?

ELD Standard:
Identify the multiple meanings of words.

ELA Standard:
Identify multiple meaning words.

Multiple Meaning Words

Read the sentences in the box.

Fill in the bubble for the sentence where the underlined word has the same meaning as the word in the sentence above.

Discuss your answers with a partner.

1. **The sun gives us _light_.**

   In which sentence does the word light mean the same thing as in the sentence above?
   - ○ The suitcase was very light.
   - ○ The light from the lamp is too bright.
   - ○ Please wear a light jacket.
   - ○ The matches won't light.

2. **That tomato is still _green_.**

   In which sentence does the word green mean the same thing as in the sentence above?
   - ○ She hit the golf ball on the green.
   - ○ I have a green coat.
   - ○ The plum is so green that I can't eat it.
   - ○ The clerk was too green to know how to do the job.

3. **Write a _note_ to the scientist.**

   In which sentence does the word note mean the same thing as in the sentence above?
   - ○ I read the note aloud.
   - ○ Be sure you note the directions.
   - ○ He played a low note on the piano.
   - ○ When she sang, she reached a high note.

4. **The first _batter_ hit a home run.**

   In which sentence does the word batter mean the same thing as in the sentence above?
   - ○ Please mix the cake batter.
   - ○ A boat that is not tied well will batter the dock.
   - ○ Is that the batter for the cookies?
   - ○ Who will be the next batter up to bat?

Word	Meaning	Context

Teacher Worksheet 7–32

Word Meaning and Context Chart

Teach students to use context to find the meaning of words. Have students write selected vocabulary from a story.

Have students use the dictionary to check the meaning of each word.

Have students write the word in the context of a sentence from the text.

ELD Standard:
Use context clues.

ELA Standard:
Use sentence and word context to find the meaning of unknown words.

Word Meaning and Context Chart

Write the vocabulary word.

Use a dictionary. Write the meaning of each word.

Write the word in the context of a sentence from the text.

Word	Meaning	Context

Word	Synonym	Sentence
amazing	surprising	It was <u>amazing</u> how many calories he ate everyday.

Teacher Worksheet 7–33

Synonym Chart

Have students use a dictionary or a thesaurus to find the synonyms for selected words. Have students write a sentence for each word. Have students read the sentences to a partner. This worksheet can be done as a daily in class or homework activity using vocabulary words from a content area selection each day.

ELD Standard:
Identify synonyms and antonyms.

ELA Standard:
Understand and explain common antonyms and synonyms.

Name_____ Date _____

Synonym Chart

Choose ten words from the story that you do not know. Find a synonym in the dictionary or thesaurus.

Word	Synonym	Sentence

Word	Picture	Synonym	Antonym	Sentence
delivers		gives	takes	The postman delivers our mail every day.

Synonym/Antonym Chart

Teach the concept of synonyms and antonyms.

A synonym is a word that means the same thing as another word.

An antonym means the opposite.

● Have students use a dictionary or thesaurus to find the synonyms and antonyms of verbs.

● Review that a verb is an action word. It tells what someone or something does.

● Have students select 10 new vocabulary verbs from the reading or content selection and complete the chart with a partner.

ELD Standard:
Identify synonyms and antonyms.

ELA Standard:
Understand and explain common antonyms and synonyms.

Synonym/Antonym Chart

Select eight verbs from the reading or content selection. Complete the chart with a partner.
Use a dictionary or thesaurus to identify a synonym and an antonym for each verb.

Sentence								
Antonym								
Synonym								
Picture								
Word								

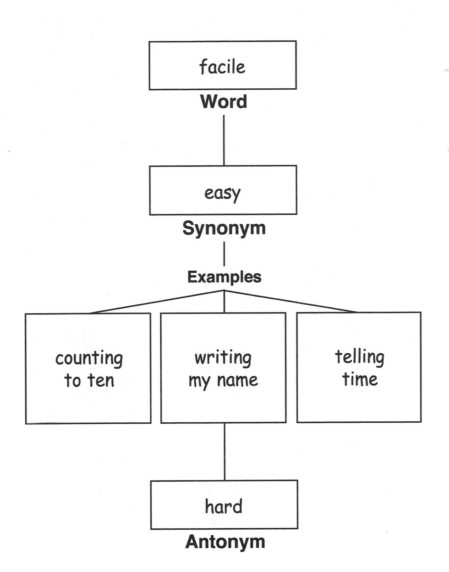

Word
facile

Synonym
easy

Examples

counting to ten

writing my name

telling time

Antonym
hard

Teacher Worksheet 7–35

Antonyms and Synonyms Concept Map

Teach students that a *synonym* is a word that has the same meaning as another word. An *antonym* means the opposite of the word.

Complete the concept map with students using vocabulary words from the reading selection.

ELD Standard:
Identify antonyms and synonyms.

ELA Standard:
Understand and explain common antonyms and synonyms.

Antonyms and Synonyms Concept Map

Use a vocabulary word to complete the chart with a partner.

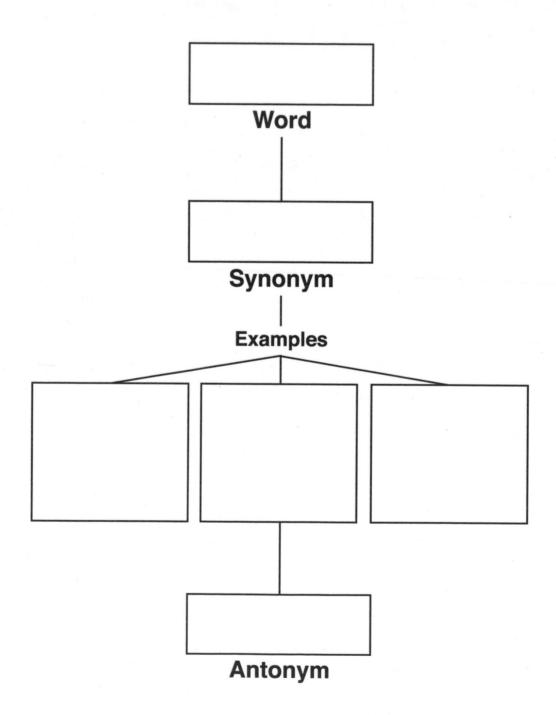

Word

Synonym

Examples

Antonym

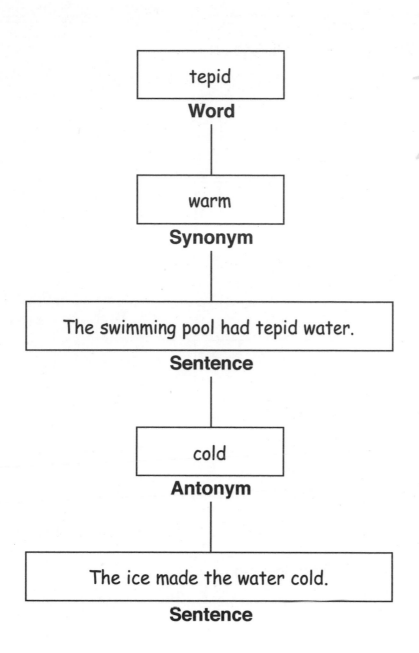

tepid
Word

warm
Synonym

The swimming pool had tepid water.
Sentence

cold
Antonym

The ice made the water cold.
Sentence

Teacher Worksheet 7–36

Antonyms and Synonyms Word Map

Teach antonyms and synonyms using this word map.

ELD Standard:
Identify antonyms and synonyms.

ELA Standard:
Understand and explain common antonyms and synonyms.

Antonyms and Synonyms Word Map

● Write a vocabulary word from the story and complete this word map.

● Read your sentences to a partner.

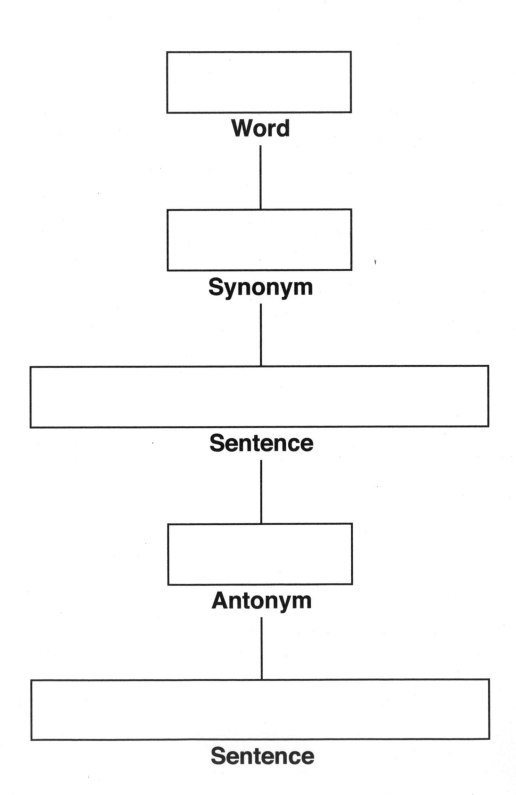

Word

Synonym

Sentence

Antonym

Sentence

Word	Part of Speech	Synonym or Definition	Sentence	Picture

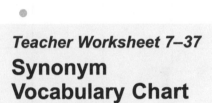

Teacher Worksheet 7–37

Synonym Vocabulary Chart

Teach students 10–13 new vocabulary words before reading a content selection. Have students list words on the chart and complete the chart with a partner.

ELD Standard:
Identify synonyms and antonyms.

ELA Standard:
Understand and explain common antonyms and synonyms.

Synonym Vocabulary Chart

●   Write the vocabulary words from the selection.

●   Complete the chart.

●   Read your sentences to a partner.

Word	Part of Speech	Synonym or Definition	Sentence	Picture

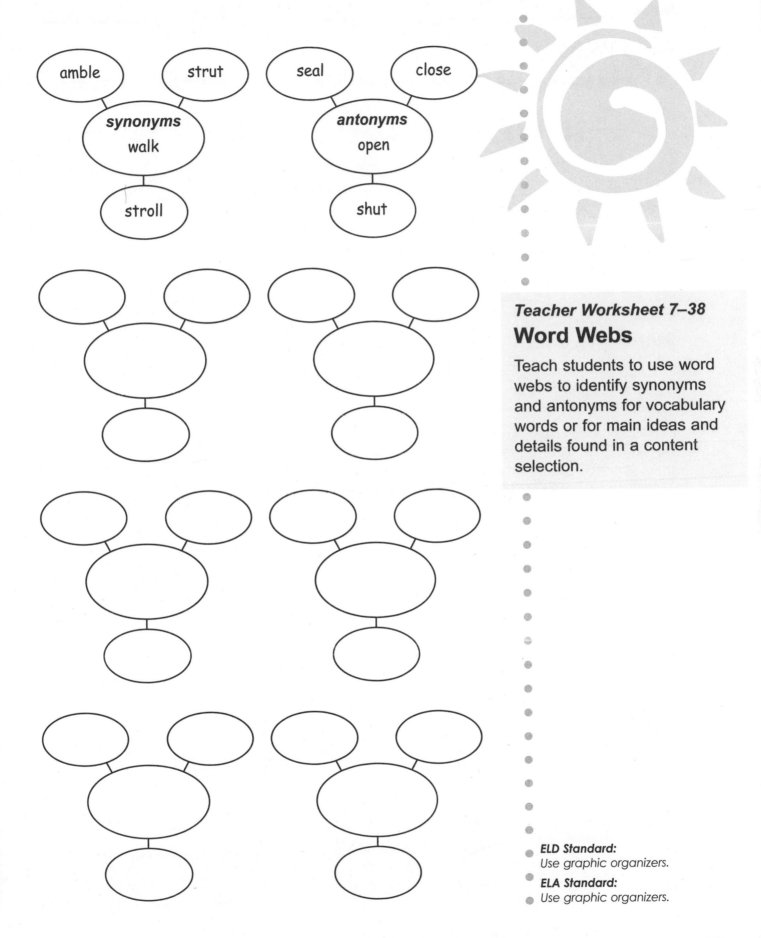

amble   **strut**

synonyms
walk

stroll

seal   **close**

antonyms
open

shut

Teacher Worksheet 7–38
Word Webs

Teach students to use word webs to identify synonyms and antonyms for vocabulary words or for main ideas and details found in a content selection.

ELD Standard:
Use graphic organizers.
ELA Standard:
Use graphic organizers.

Word Webs

Choose six words from the text selection. Write synonyms or antonyms for the six words.

synonyms

antonyms

synonyms

antonyms

synonyms

antonyms

Materials

- [ ] paper
- [ ] felt markers
- [ ] dictionary/thesaurus
- [ ] colored construction paper

Directions

- Give each student a new word.
- Students write and illustrate the word.
- Students write a synonym for the word.
- Students write the definition on the back of the picture.
- Students describe their drawing to a partner and read the definition to him/her.
- Students write their own sentences using the word under the definition.
- Post pictures around the room.

Side One

Illustrate the word **task**:   Write a synonym:

Side Two

Definition: _____

_____

Synonym: _____

Sentence: _____

_____

Teacher Worksheet 7–39

Making Pictures, Creating Meaning

Teach students to create meaning with pictures. This technique helps students to learn the meaning of new words by creating a picture that has personal meaning.

ELD Standard:
Identify synonyms and antonyms.

ELA Standard:
Understand and explain common antonyms and synonyms.

Making Pictures, Creating Meaning

This technique helps students to learn the meaning of new words by creating a picture that has personal meaning.

Use paper, felt markers, dictionary/thesaurus or colored paper.

Directions

- Write 5 new words on five index cards. Draw a picture for each word.
- Write a synonym, a definition, and a sentence for each word on the other side of the index card.
- Describe your drawing to a partner. Read the definition to him/her.
- Post your pictures around the room.

Side One

Illustrate the word _____: Write the word:

```
┌─────────────┐
│             │
│             │
│             │
│             │
│             │
└─────────────┘
```

Side Two

Definition: _____

_____

Synonym: _____

Sentence: _____

_____

All Things Are Made of Matter

All the things around you are made of matter. Matter is anything that has weight and takes up space. There are three types of matter: *solids, liquids* and *gases.* Solids have a definite shape. Solids also take up a definite amount of space. A desk, a book and a bicycle are all solids. Liquids are the second type of matter. Liquids take up a definite amount of space. Liquids, however, have no definite shape. They take on the shape of a container. Water, milk, and juice are liquids. Gases are the third type of matter. Gases lack a definite shape. Gases take up different amounts of space. Air and propane are gases.

Use these vocabulary words.

hot chocolate	house	breeze	book	milk
air in a balloon	leaf	rain	desk	hamburger
juice	air	soda	wind	fish

Solid	Liquid	Gas

1. What is a solid?

   _____

2. What solids do you eat?

   _____

3. What is a liquid?

   _____

4. What liquids do you drink?

   _____

5. What is a gas?

   _____

6. What type of matter do we use to blow up a balloon?

   _____

Teacher Worksheet 7–40

Categorization and Context

Have students read the questions first and then read the passage.

Have students fill in the chart, classifying each word as a **solid**, **liquid**, or **gas**.

Have students ask and answer the questions with a partner.

Teach the concept of different types of matter. Use a rock, a glass of water and a balloon to demonstrate a solid, a liquid and a gas.

ELD Standard:
Ask and answer simple questions.

ELA Standard:
Categorize groups of words.

All Things Are Made of Matter

All the things around you are made of matter. Matter is anything that has weight and takes up space. There are three types of matter: *solids, liquids* and *gases*. Solids have a definite shape. Solids also take up a definite amount of space. A desk, a book, and a bicycle are all solids. Liquids are the second type of matter. Liquids take up a definite amount of space. Liquids, however, have no definite shape. They take on the shape of a container. Water, milk, and juice are liquids. Gases are the third type of matter. Gases lack a definite shape. Gases take up different amounts of space. Air and propane are gases.

Use these vocabulary words.

hot chocolate	house	breeze	book	milk
air in a balloon	leaf	rain	desk	hamburger
juice	air	soda	wind	fish

Solid	Liquid	Gas

1. What is a solid?

   _____

2. What solids do you eat?

   _____

3. What is a liquid?

   _____

4. What liquids do you drink?

   _____

5. What is a gas?

   _____

6. What type of matter do we use to blow up a balloon?

   _____

Middle School
High School
Vocabulary Building Activities

Standards-based

Word	Context	Meaning

Teacher Worksheet 7–41

Vocabulary Words in Context

Have students identify words that need clarifying in the text.

Have students write the sentences in which the words are found.

Teach students how to use context clues:

Tell students to ask themselves the following questions:

1. *What clues do the words around the word give me?*

2. *How is the word used in the sentence?*

3. *What clues do the other words in the sentences give me?*

ELD Standard:
Use context clues.

ELA Standard:
Use sentence and word context to find the meaning of unknown words.

Name_____ Date _____

Vocabulary Words in Context

✓ Identify the words that need clarifying in the text.

✓ Find the sentences in the text that contain these words. Write the sentences.

✓ Use content clues to identify the meanings of the words in the subject-area selection.

✓ Look up the words in the dictionary.

Word	Context	Meaning

Page	Word	Word Meaning	Word in Context of a Sentence from the Text	My Original Sentence

Teacher Worksheet 7–42

Vocabulary Journal
Vocabulary in Context

● Have students write 10 vocabulary words from the subject area selection.

● Use the **Rule of 3** to teach students the words.

● Have students use vocabulary words from the reading selection and complete the vocabulary journal.

Explain the term <u>in context</u> as the text that surrounds a word or phrase that helps to explain a word's meaning.

ELD Standard:
Use context clues.

ELA Standard:
Use sentences and word context to find the meaning of unknown words.

Vocabulary Journal: *Vocabulary in Context*

Write 10 words from the subject area selection

Complete the vocabulary page with a partner.

Page	Word	Word Meaning	Word in Context of a Sentence from the Text	My Original Sentence

Word	Sentence from Text	Dictionary Definition

Teacher Worksheet 7–43

Words in Context Chart

● Teach students to use context to help define a word's meaning.

● Review the use of a dictionary and alphabetical order.

● Choose ten vocabulary words from the text and have students complete the chart with a partner.

ELD Standard:
Use context clues.

ELA Standard:
Use sentences and word context to find the meaning of unknown words.

Words in Context

Select eight vocabulary words from the content selection.

Dictionary Definition								
Sentence from Text								
Word								

Vocabulary Word	Related Words
friendly	amicable, nice
antique	old, 18th century
categorize	map, graph

Name_____ Date _____

Related Words Chart

✓ Write 14 vocabulary words from the subject area selection.

✓ Write words that are related.

Example 1: dog (related words: cat, mouse) These words are related because they all are animals.

Example 2: amicable (nice, friendly) These words are related because they all are synonyms.

Vocabulary Word	Related Words

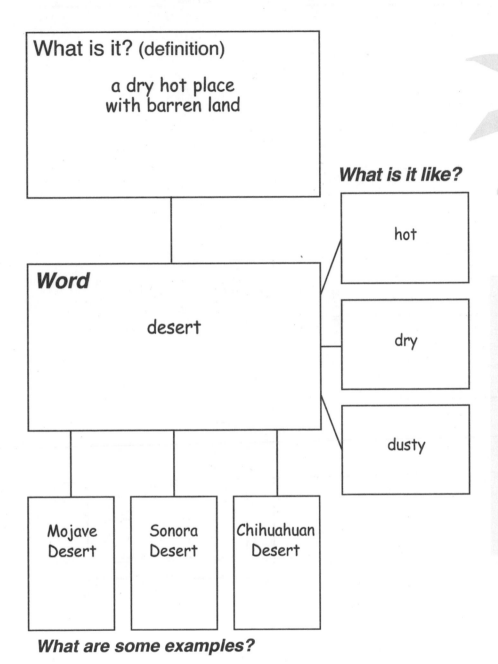

What is it? (definition)

a dry hot place
with barren land

What is it like?

hot

Word

desert

dry

dusty

Mojave
Desert

Sonora
Desert

Chihuahuan
Desert

What are some examples?

Teacher Worksheet 7–45

Word Map

Teach students to use a word map to clarify word meaning. Have students choose a word they don't know from the text selection. Have students find the definition of the word in the dictionary.

Then have students describe and give examples of the word.

ELD Standard:
Use graphic organizers.

ELA Standard:
Use graphic organizers.

Word Map

Use this word map to clarify word meaning.

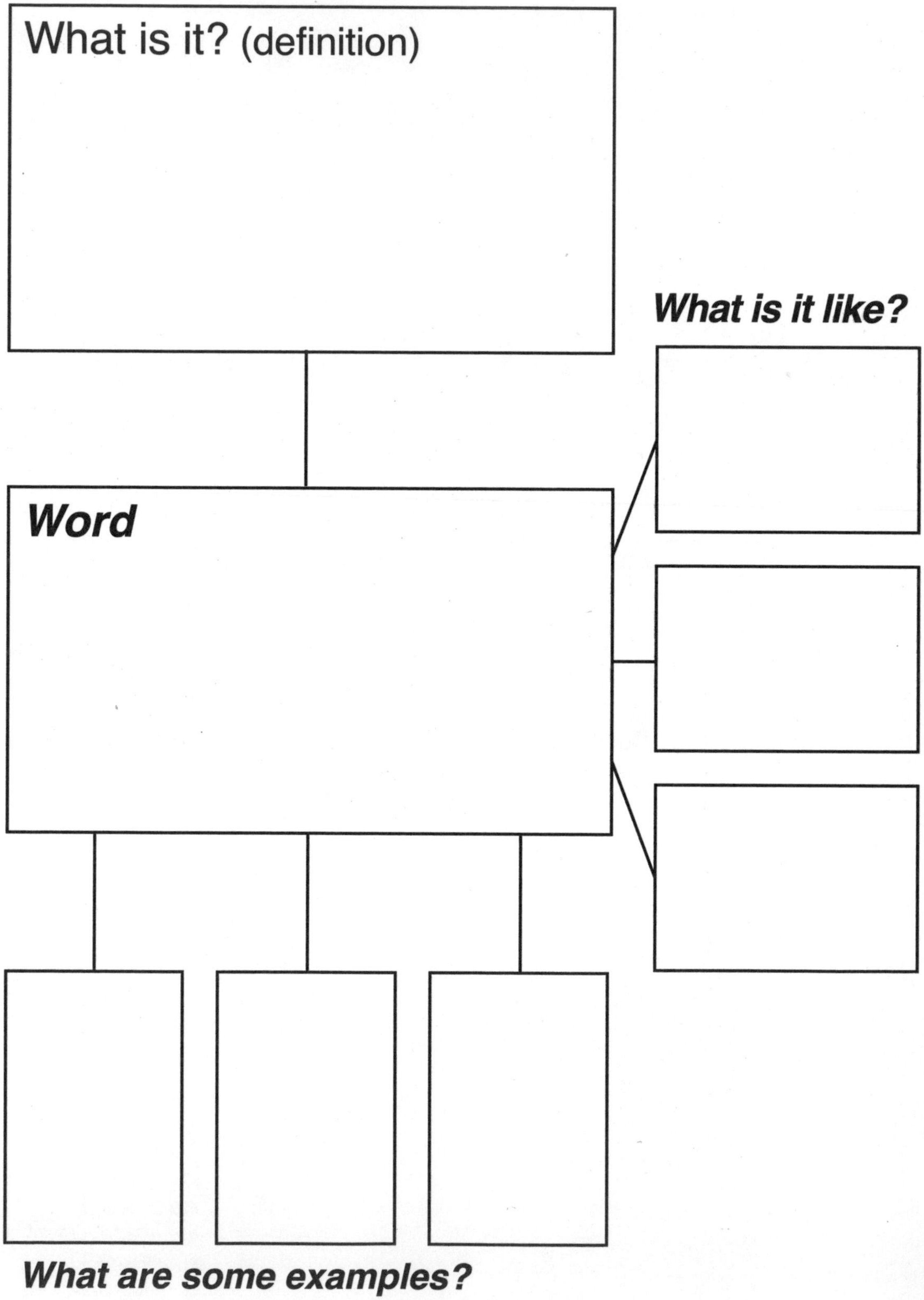

What is it? (definition)

What is it like?

Word

What are some examples?

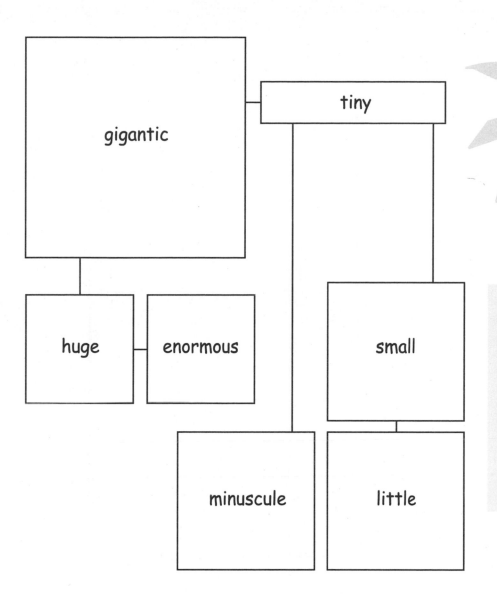

gigantic

tiny

huge

enormous

small

minuscule

little

Teacher Worksheet 7–46

Word Web

Teach students to use this word web to brainstorm synonyms, then a synonym for those synonyms as you go around the web.

Have students do the same thing with antonyms.

ELD Standard:
Use graphic organizers.

ELA Standard:
Use graphic organizers.

Word Web

✓ Use this word web to brainstorm synonyms, then a synonym
   for that synonym as you go around the web.

✓ You can do the same thing with antonyms.

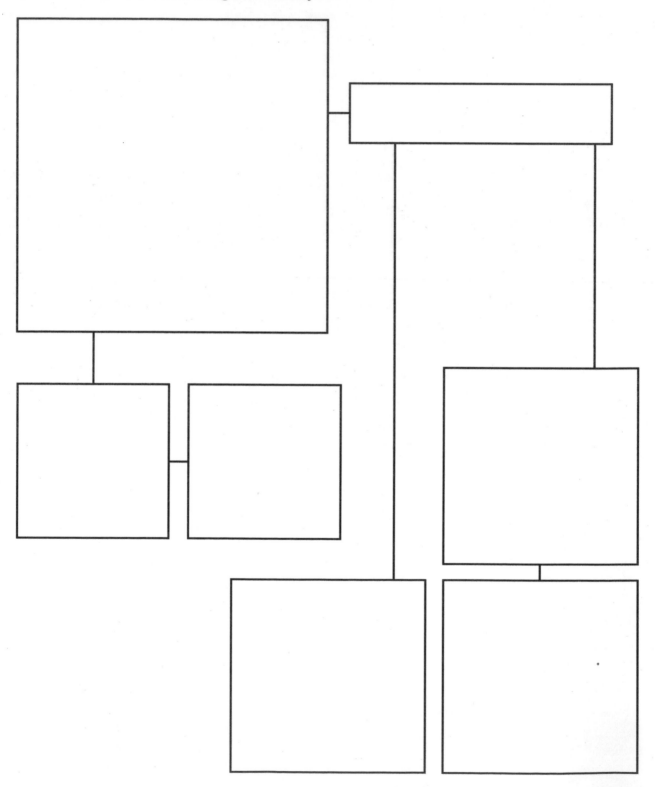

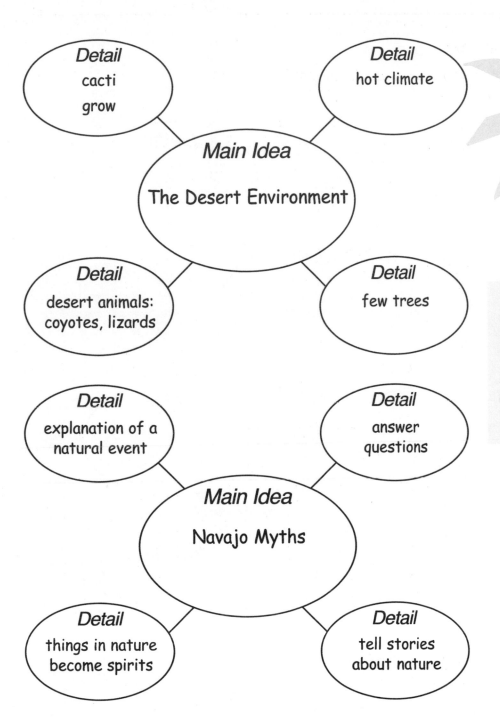

Detail
cacti
grow

Detail
hot climate

Main Idea
The Desert Environment

Detail
desert animals:
coyotes, lizards

Detail
few trees

Detail
explanation of a
natural event

Detail
answer
questions

Main Idea
Navajo Myths

Detail
things in nature
become spirits

Detail
tell stories
about nature

Main Idea Word Web

Use this word web for main ideas and details in a story.

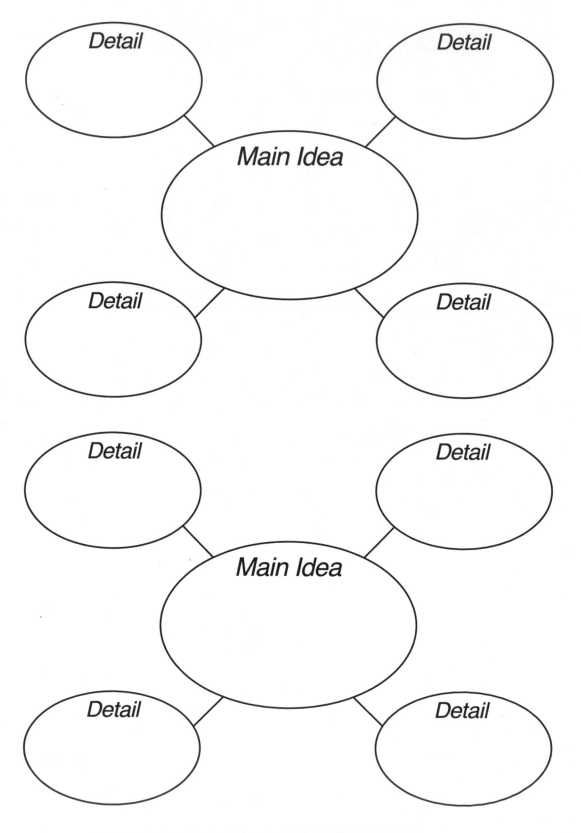

Word	Situations or Events (context)
camouflaged	The soldier went toward the village. He was <u>camouflaged</u> by his uniform which was the color of the bushes around him.

Teacher Worksheet 7–48
Vocabulary Chart

Teach students how to find word meaning using context clues.

Have students list words in a paragraph they don't know.

Have students ask: **How do the other words and sentences in the paragraph help me understand the meaning of the word?**

Use this vocabulary chart to list the vocabulary words from a content selection.

Then list the situations, events or context in which the word is found.

ELD Standard:
Identify words in context.

ELA Standard:
Use sentence and word context to find the meaning of unknown words.

Name_____ Date _____

Vocabulary Chart

Use this vocabulary chart to list the vocabulary words from a content selection.
Then list the situations, events or context in which the word is found.

Word	Situations or Events (context)

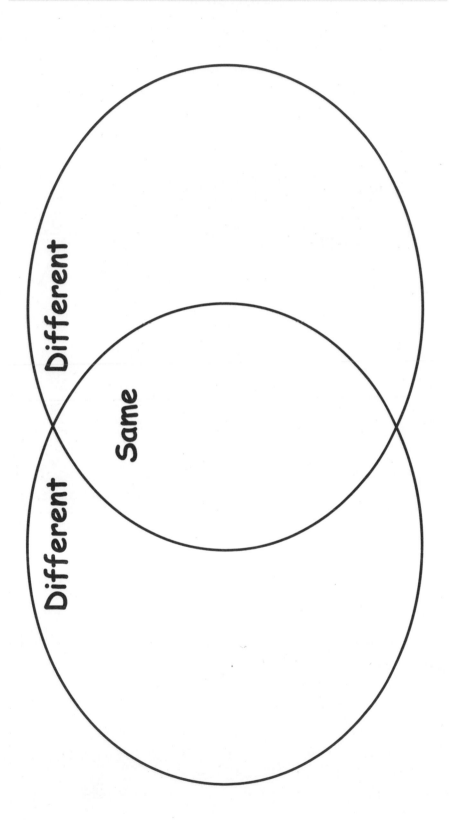

Different

Different

Same

Teacher Worksheet 7–49
Compare and Contrast with the Venn Diagram

Teach students to use the Venn Diagram to compare and contrast stories, characters or settings. Use a simple topic to start like apples and bananas. Have students fill in the Venn diagram. Use concepts with older students like comparing and contrasting inventions of the 20th and 21st centuries.

ELD Standard:
Use graphic organizers.

ELA Standard:
Use graphic organizers.

Compare and Contrast with the Venn Diagram

Use the Venn Diagram to compare and contrast stories, characters, or settings.

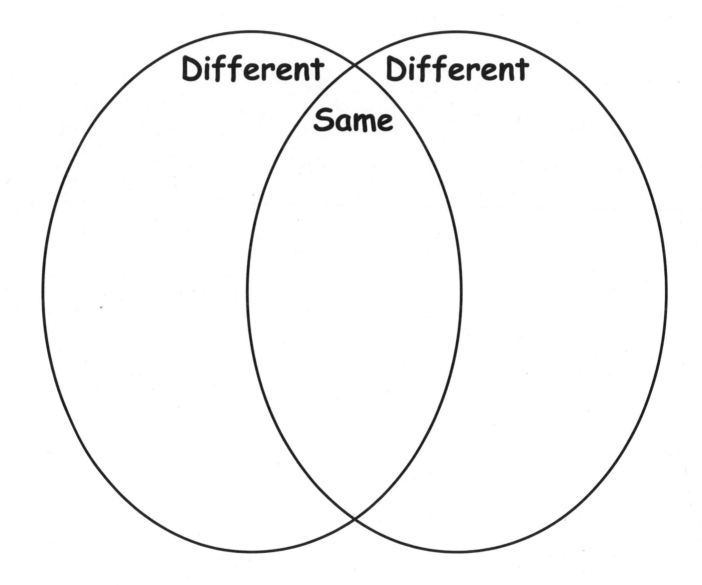

Nouns	Verbs	Adjectives	Prepositions

Teacher Worksheet 7–50

Personal Vocabulary Journals

Team Vocabulary Walls

Have students keep their own permanent personal vocabulary journals.

• Have students write 10 to 15 new words every day.

• Have students write sentences using the words.

Develop Team Vocabulary Walls and have teams of students present:

• Words for the day

• Words for the week

• Create a Word Wall using words from a subject area selection. Categorize words by parts of speech.

ELD Standard:
Identify parts of speech.

ELA Standard:
Identify and correctly use various parts of speech.

Personal Vocabulary Journals

Team Vocabulary Walls

Keep your own permanent personal vocabulary journals.

✓ Write 10 to 15 new words every day.

✓ Categorize the words by the parts of speech.

Write a sentence for each word. Read the sentences to a partner.

Nouns	Verbs	Adjectives	Prepositions

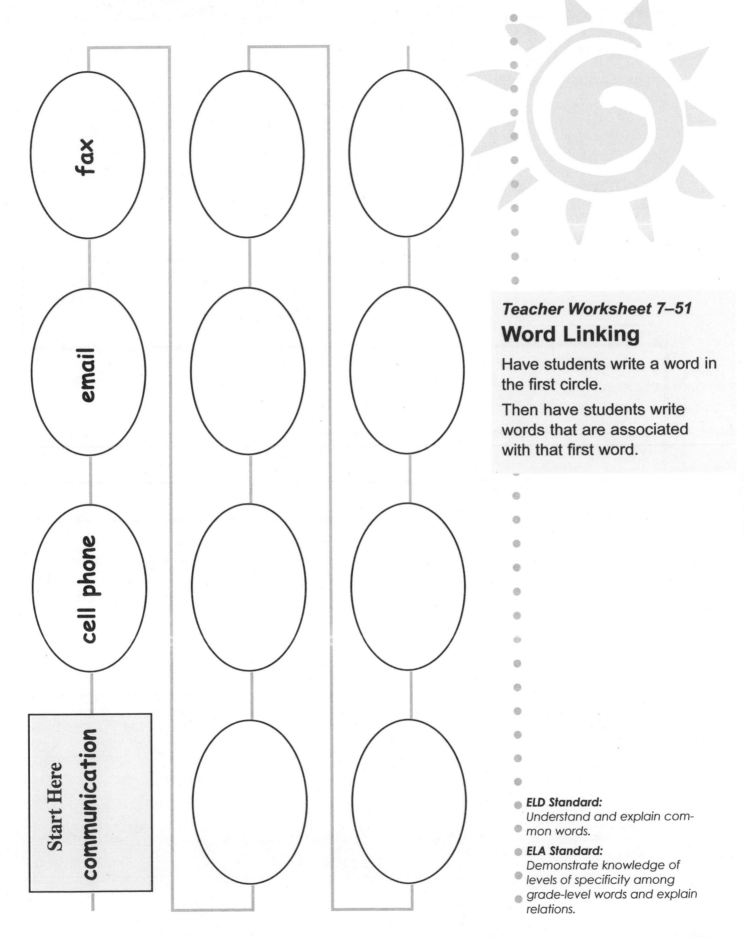

fax

email

cell phone

Start Here
communication

Word Linking

Have students write a word in the first circle.

Then have students write words that are associated with that first word.

ELD Standard:
Understand and explain common words.

ELA Standard:
Demonstrate knowledge of levels of specificity among grade-level words and explain relations.

Word Linking

Write a word in the first circle.

Then write words that are associated with that first word.

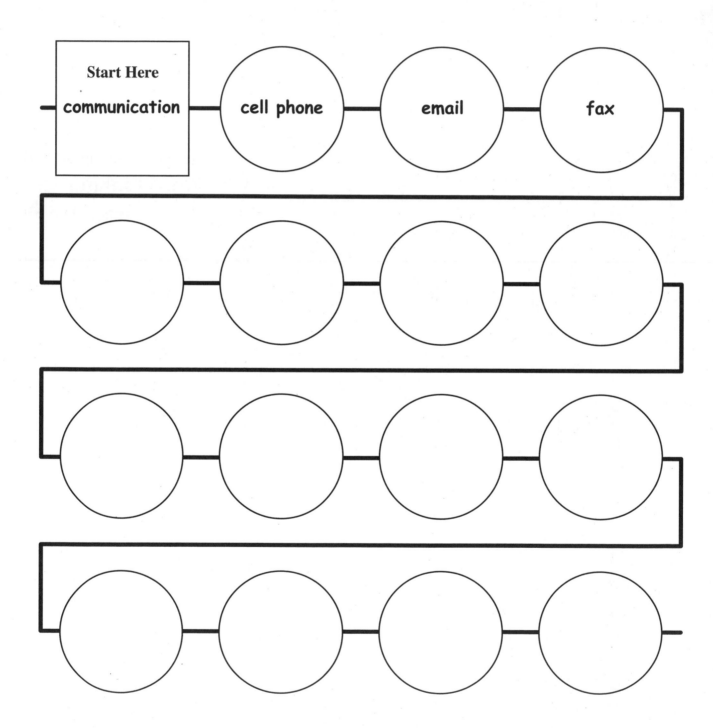

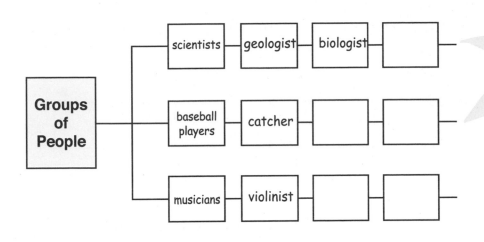

Groups of People
- scientists → geologist → biologist → ☐
- baseball players → catcher → ☐ → ☐
- musicians → violinist → ☐ → ☐

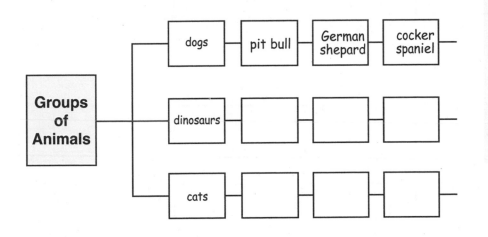

Groups of Animals
- dogs → pit bull → German shepard → cocker spaniel
- dinosaurs → ☐ → ☐ → ☐
- cats → ☐ → ☐ → ☐

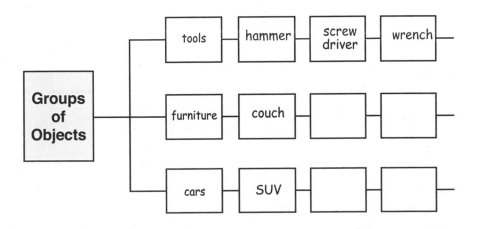

Groups of Objects
- tools → hammer → screw driver → wrench
- furniture → couch → ☐ → ☐
- cars → SUV → ☐ → ☐

Teacher Worksheet 7–52

Categorizing Vocabulary Words in Groups

Teach categorization by linking words that illustrate concepts.

ELD Standard:
Understand and explain common words.

ELA Standard:
Demonstrate knowledge of levels of specificity among grade-level appropriate words and explain relations.

Categorizing Vocabulary Words in Groups

Complete the chart with a partner.

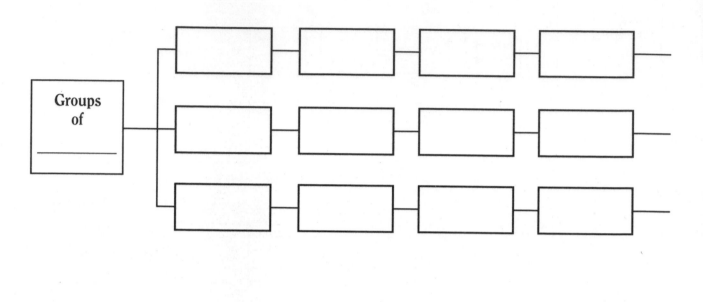

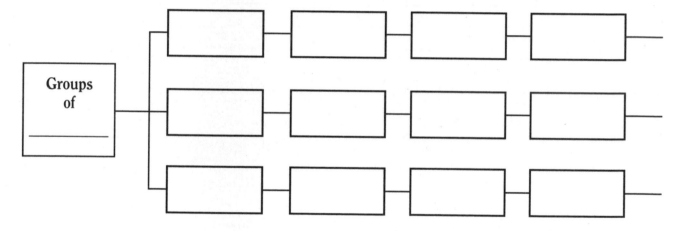

Circle of Life

This activity is used to graph out important events in a person's life and is an excellent prewriting activity. It can be used alone or with the nine squares sheet, and is a great way to lead English Language Learners into the process of writing about an autobiographical incident. First, the teacher models the entire process using a personal experience as an example.

These are the steps:

1. Draw a large circle on the board.
2. Divide the circle into sections representing different ages or stages of life.
3. Draw pictures of significant personal events that occurred within each time span.
4. Describe and act out each event to aid student comprehension.
5. Afterward, circle one specific event that you plan to illustrate in detail using the Nine Squares sheet.
6. Moving sequentially from square to square, illustrate the events that make up the specific incident that was selected in the Circle of Life. Then add text (a word, a phrase, a sentence or paragraph) to each square.
7. From this, write out a description of the autobiographical incident.
8. Finally, students begin the process by starting their own Circle of Life. A student handout master is included on the following page

Circle of Life and Nine Squares Activities

Teacher Instructions

by permission:
***Project Write** 1999*

ELD Standard:
Write a narrative.

ELA Standard:
Write descriptions that use concrete sensory details.

Circle of Life

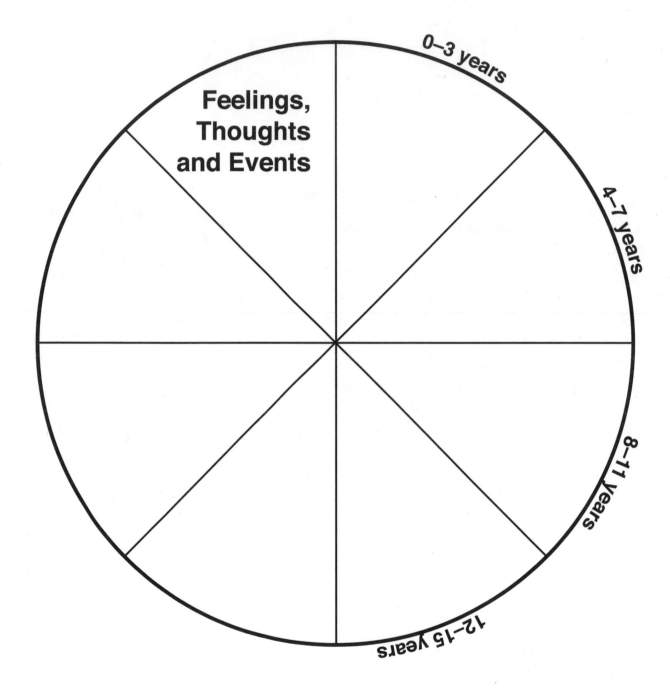

Feelings,
Thoughts
and Events

0–3 years

4–7 years

8–11 years

12–15 years

Storyboarding

Storyboarding is a technique used in animation, advertising and other fields to match dialogue and visuals. It's also a great way for students with limited English writing ability to show their comprehension of a story. Have students divide a blank, unlined piece of paper, into 6, 8 or 10 squares. In each square, students draw *in sequence* the major events that took place in the story. Drawings should be detailed and colorful! Beneath each picture, students write, according to their ability, some text (e.g., a description, quote) to accompany the drawings. Some students may be able to write only one word, others may write several sentences. Students can also copy relevant sections of the text to place beneath their drawings. A blank master for storyboards is included on page 210.

A blank master for storyboards is included on page 210.

Storyboarding
Teacher Instructions

Example:

ELD Standard:
Write a narrative.

ELA Standard:
Write descriptions that use concrete sensory details.

Variation of Story Boards

Story Impressions Strategy: Using the Rule of 3

The "Story Impressions Strategy" (McGinley and Denner 1987) helps students internalize the meaning of vocabulary words before reading a published story. These are the steps for implementing this strategy:

1. The teacher chooses 5 to 10 key words from a story or expository passage and lists them in the order that they appear.

2. The words are written vertically on a whiteboard or an overhead projector.

3. Word meanings are discussed using Rules 1 and 2 of the **Rule of 3**. The students discuss the words and their meanings. They spell and say the words. They tell the meaning of each word to a partner. They use word analysis to label each word's part of speech.

4. Rule 3, or deep processing, is done by having groups of students compose a story using the words in the exact order that they are written on the whiteboard or overhead.

5. The students create a storyboard. They write sentences under the pictures that contain the vocabulary words.

Storyboard

Storyboard

Create a storyboard for
a story you have read.

ELD Standard:
Write a narrative.

ELA Standard:
*Write descriptions that use
concrete, sensory details.*

Storyboards

Storyboard			

Use a Reading Selection

Directions:

(This technique also can be used with student writings.)

- Students read a subject area selection.
- Students write a sentence or quote from the selection on a piece of white paper.
- Students illustrate the quote.

Use Student Summaries

Directions:

- Students summarize a selection.
- Students read their summary to a partner.
- The partner picks a sentence or quote from the summary to illustrate.

Make a Collage

Directions:

- Students choose several sentences from a subject area selection.
- Students make a collage of drawings to illustrate the sentences.

Teacher Worksheet 7–54

Subject Quotes

Have students write quotes from subject area selections. Have students illustrate quotes to help them derive meaning.

ELD Standard:
Write a short narrative.

ELA Standard:
Write a narrative.

Name_____ Date _____

Pictures and Story Quotes

● Write quotes from the reading selection.
● Draw a picture to illustrate each quote.
● Read the quote and explain your picture to a partner.

Title of Story

Author

Quote from the story:

Picture

Quote from the story:

Picture

Simile	Two unlike things being compared	Meaning	Illustration
His mouth was <u>as dry as a bone</u>.			
His hands were <u>as cold as ice</u>.			
Mary's smile was <u>as bright as a button</u>.			
The good grade on his exam made Jose <u>as proud as a peacock</u>.			
The reply was <u>as bold as brass</u>.			

Worksheet 7–55

Similes

Teach similes as a comparison of two things using *like* or *as.*

Use poems with similes.

Discuss why writers use similes.

ELD Standard:
Identify similes and metaphors.

ELA Standard:
Identify significant literacy devices similes, metaphors, symbolism, irony.

Simile Chart

Simlies are a comparison of two things using _like_ or _as_.

Simile	Two unlike things being compared	Meaning	Illustration
His mouth was <u>as dry</u> <u>as a bone</u>.			
His hands were <u>as cold as ice</u>.			
Mary's smile was <u>as bright as a button</u>.			
The good grade on his exam made Jose <u>as proud</u> <u>as a peacock</u>.			
The reply was <u>as bold as brass</u>.			

Base	Meaning	Example Words	Origin
act	to act	**act**ive	Latin
acu, acr, ac	needle	**acu**puncture	Latin
alt	high	**alt**itude	Latin
anima, anim	life, mind	**anim**al	Latin
ann, enn	year	**ann**ual	Latin
anthrop	man	**anthrop**ology	Greek
aqua	water	**aqua**tics	Latin
arm	army, weapon	**arm**y	Latin
arbitr, arbiter	to judge, consider	**arbitr**ator	Latin
art	craft, skill	**art**ist	Latin
arthr, art	segment, joint	**arthr**itis	Greek
aud	to hear	**aud**ible	Latin
biblio, bibl	book	**biblio**graphy	Greek
bio	life	**bio**logy	Greek
capit, cipit	head	**capit**al	Latin
caus	cause, case, lawsuit	**caus**e	Latin
cede	to go, yield	inter**cede**	Latin
cele	honor	**cele**brate	Latin
cent	one hundred	**cent**ury	Latin
cept, capt, cip, cap, ceive, ceipt	to take, hold, grasp	inter**cept**	Latin
cert	sure, to trust	**cert**ify	Latin
circ, circum	around	**circ**uit	Latin
cog	to know	**cog**nitive	Latin
dem	people	**dem**ocracy	Greek
dent, odont	tooth	**ortho**dontist	Greek
dic, dict	to say, to speak, assert	**dic**tation	Latin
ethn	nation	**ethn**icity	Greek

Worksheet 7–56

Greek and Latin Roots

Have students write two words for each Greek or Latin root. Have students use the words in a sentence. Then have students create a paragraph using ten of the words.

● **ELD Standard:**
Use Greek and Latin roots.

● **ELA Standard:**
Use knowledge of Greek, Latin, and Anglo-Saxon roots and affixes to understand content area vocabulary.

Use Greek and Latin Roots

Use knowledge of Greek, Latin, and Anglo-Saxon roots and affixes to understand content area vocabulary.

Base	Meaning	Sample Words	Origin
act	to act	**act**ive	Latin
acu, acr, ac	needle	**acu**puncture	Latin
alt	high	**alt**itude	Latin
anima, anim	life, mind	**anim**al	Latin
ann, enn	year	**ann**ual	Latin
anthrop	man	**anthrop**ology	Greek
aqua	water	**aqua**tics	Latin
arm	army, weapon	**arm**y	Latin
arbitr, arbiter	to judge, consider	**arbitr**ator	Latin
art	craft, skill	**art**ist	Latin
arthr, art	segment, joint	**arthr**itis	Greek
aud	to hear	**aud**ible	Latin
biblio, bibl	book	**biblio**graphy	Greek
bio	life	**bio**logy	Greek
capit, cipit	head	**capit**al	Latin
caus	cause, case, lawsuit	**caus**e	Latin
cede	to go, yield	inter**cede**	Latin
cele	honor	**cele**brate	Latin
cent	one hundred	**cent**ury	Latin
cept, capt, cip, cap, ceive, ceipt	to take, hold, grasp	inter**cept**	Latin
cert	sure, to trust	**cert**ify	Latin
circ, circum	around	**circ**uit	Latin
cog	to know	**cog**nitive	Latin
dem	people	**dem**ocracy	Greek
dent, odont	tooth	**ortho**dontist	Greek
dic, dict	to say, to speak, assert	**dic**tation	Latin
ethn	nation	**ethn**icity	Greek

100 Most Commonly Misspelled Words in English

acceptable	fiery	occasionally
accidentally	foreign	occurrence
accommodate	gauge	pastime
acquire	grateful	perseverance
acquit	guarantee	personnel
a lot	harass	playwright
amateur	height	possession
apparent	hierarchy	precede
argument	humorous	principal/principle
atheist	ignorance	privilege
bellwether	immediate	pronunciation
calendar	independent	publicity
category	indispensable	questionnaire
cemetery	inoculate	receive/receipt
changeable	intelligence	recommend
collectible	its / it's	reference
column	jewelry	referred
committed	judgment	relevant
conscience	kernel	restaurant
conscientious	liaison	rhyme
conscious	library	rhythm
consensus	license	schedule
definite	lightning	separate
diligent	maintenance	sergeant
discipline	maneuver	supersede
dumbbell	medieval	their/they're/there
dungeon	memento	threshold
embarrassment	millennium	twelfth
equipment	miniature	tyranny
exceed	minuscule	until
exhilarate	misspell	vacuum
existence	neighbor	weather
experience	noticeable	weird

Spanish Cognates

Many words in Spanish resemble words in English. The following cognates provide the Spanish-speaking student a quick source of building an English vocabulary. However, it should be noted that not all words that sound or look alike in English and Spanish have the same meaning.

A

abandon - abandonar
abdicate - abdicar
abnormal - abnormal
abolition - abolición
abominable - abominable
abrupt - abrupto
absolute - absoluto
abolutely - absolutamente
absorb - absorber
abstraction - abstracción
absurd - absurdo
abundant - abundante
abunantly - abundantemente
abuse(n) - abuso
academy - academia
accelerate - acelerar

B

bayonet - bayoneta
benediction - bendición
benefice - beneficio
benefit - beneficio
benevolence - benevolencia
benevolent - benévolo
benign - benigno

biblical - bíblico
bicycle - bicicleta
biography - biografía
boot - bota

C

calculate - calcular
calendar - calendario
calm (v.) - calmar
calvary - calvario
combine - combinar
camel - camello

D

defect - defecto
direct - directo
distinct - distinto

E

echo - eco
edict - edicto
edifice - edificio
effect - efecto
efficacy - eficacia
elector - elector
elegant - elegante

empire - imperio
enemy - enemigo
enigma - enigma
envy - envidia
episode - episodio
error - error
essence - esencia
essential - esencial
establish - establecer
eternal - eterno
eternity - eternidad

F

fabulous - fabuloso
facility - facilidad
factor - factor
faculty - facultad
false - falso
falsify - falsear
fame - fama
family - familia
famous - famoso
fascinate - fascinar
fatality - fatalidad
fatigue - fatiga
favorable - favorable

G

gallant - galante
gallop - galope
gardener - jardinero
gas - gas
gasoline - gasolina
generosity - generosidad
genteel - gentil
genuine - genuino
germ - germen
gesture - gesto
giant - gigante
glacial - glacial
globe - globo
glorious - glorioso
glory - gloria
golf - golf
gradual - gradual
gratitude - gratitud
grotesque - grotesco

H

habitual - habitual
hatchet - hacha
heir - heredero
hemisphere - hemisferio
herb - hierba
hereditary - hereditario
historian - historiador
history - historia
honor - honor
horizontal - horizontal
horrendous - horrendo
horrible - horrible
horror - horror

hospitality - hospitalidad
hostile - hostil

I

idea - idea
ideal - ideal
identity - identidad
idiot - idiota
ignorant - ignorante
illuminate - iluminar
image - imagen
imaginary - imaginario
imaginative - imaginativo
imagine - imaginar
immediate - inmediato
immediately - inmediatamente
immense - inmenso

J

jar - jarra
jargon - jerga
judicial - judicial
judiciary - judiciario
just - justo

K

kilogram - kilogramo

L

labor (n) - labor
labor (v) - laborar
laboratory - laboratorio
laborious - laborioso
lament - lamentar
latitude - latitud

legal - legal
legislator - legislador
legumes - legumbres
liberal - liberal
liberty - libertad
limit - limitar
line - línea

M

magistrate - magistrado
magnitude - magnitud
majesty - majestad
malice - malicia
malignant - maligno
mandate - mandato
manner - manera
manual - manual
manuscript - manuscrito
map - mapa
march (v) - marchar
margin - margen
marine - marino
mark (n) - marca
mark (v) - marcar

N

narrate - narrar
natal - natal
national - nacional
nationality - nacionalidad
native - nativo
natural - natural
naturally - naturalmente
naval - naval
navigable - navegable

necessary - necesario
necessity - necesidad
negative - negativo
nerve - nervio

O

oasis - oasis
obedience - obediencia
obedient - obediente
object - objeto
objective - objetivo
oblige - obligar
obscure - obscuro
observe - observar
obstruct - obstruir
obtain - obtener

P

pacific - pacífico
pact - pacto
palace - palacio
palm - palma
passive - pasivo
past - pasado
pasta - pasta
pastor - pastor
paternal - paterno
patience - paciencia
patio - patio

Q

quarter - cuarto
quiet - quieto
quietude - quietud

R

race(n) - raza
radiant - radiante
radiator - radiador
radical - radical
ranch - rancho
rapidity - rapidez
rare - raro
ray - rayo
realist - realista
reality - realidad
reason(v) - razonar

S

salad - ensalada
salary - salario
sanctity - santidad
sane - sano
scene - escena
second - segundo
secret(n) - secreto
secretly - secretamente
sect - secta
secular - secular
security - seguridad

T

tact - tacto
talent - talento
tamale - tamal
tardy - tardío
tariff - tarifa
tarragon - estragón
tart - tarta

tea - té
teapot - tetera
telescope - telescopio
temperature - temperaturea

U

ulterior - ulterior
ultimate - último
united - unido
unity - unidad
universal - universal
unjust - injusto
unstable - inestable
urbane - urbano
urgency - urgencia
urgent - urgente

V

vacant - vacante
vacation - vacaciones
vacillate - vacilar
vague - vago
valor - valor
vanity - vanidad
vary - variar
vast - vasto
vehicle - vehículo
vein - vena

Interdisciplinary Vocabulary Development: The Rule of 3

Words with Multiple Meanings

The following are some of the most common words with multiple meanings. You must figure out the meaning of a multiple meaning word in the context of the sentence.

Example: **Multiple Meaning Word** *can*

Meaning #1 She ***can*** lift the box all by herself.

Meaning #2 We bought a ***can*** of peas.

Oftentimes a multiple meaning word will have a different meaning when it is a noun or a verb.

Meaning #1 They want to play on the ***slide***. (noun)

Meaning #2 They ***slide*** down the hill on the sled. (verb)

A	blaze	chain	current	family	**G**
accent	blind	chamber	cushion	fan	gag
account	block	chance	cut	fast	game
ace	blow	change		fault	gauge
act	bluff	charge	**D**	feature	gear
add	board	charter	date	feel	general
address	body	check	deal	fence	get
advance	bolt	chip	degree	field	give
age	bond	choice	deposit	figure	grade
air	bore	chorus	design	file	grain
alarm	bottom	circle	dial	fill	ground
ask	bound	circuit	diamond	filter	gutter
associate	bow	clash	die	find	
attention	box	claw	dip	finish	**H**
average	brace	clear	direct	fit	habit
	brand	club	double	fix	hail
B	brush	coat	draft	flare	hall
baby	buckle	code	draw	flat	hand
back	burn	colony	dress	flight	harbor
bail	button	cool	drop	flock	hard
balance		copy	dry	flop	head
band	**C**	cord		flush	heart
bar	cabinet	course	**E**	focus	heel
bare	cable	court	element	foil	help
base	cake	crack	entry	follow	hit
bat	call	crane	even	foot	hitch
batter	cap	credit	excuse	force	hold
bear	capital	crest	express	forge	hollow
bearing	cart	crop	eye	form	home
beat	case	cross		foul	hood
bed	cast	crown	**F**	frame	hook
behind	cause	cry	face	free	horn
bill	cement	culture	fair	fund	house
bite	center	cure	fall	fuse	hull

I
ice
inflate
interest
iron
issue

J
jack
jam
jar
judge
jump
junior

K
keep
key
kick
king
knock
knot

L
land
lark
launch
law
lead
leave
let
level
lick
lie
life
light
line
live
load
lock
lodge
long
look
lot
low

M
mad
make
mark
mask

mat
mean
meet
melt
mess
mind
mine
minor
minute
miss
mix
model
mold
motion
mount
move

N
name
natural
near
need
needle
negative
nest
net
neutral
nose
note
notice
number
nurse

O
object
odd
open
order

P
pace
pack
pad
page
palm
part
particular
party
patch
pay
peak

peel
perform
picture
piece
pile
pin
pinch
pipe
pit
pitch
place
plain
plane
play
plot
plug
point
pool
pore
positive
post
power
practice
preserve
press
pressure
pride
print
pump
push
put

Q
quarter

R
race
raise
ram
range
rank
rare
rattle
reach
read
reason
record
reel
reference
reflect
register

relief
reserve
resource
respect
rest
return
reverse
review
ride
rig
right
ring
rock
roll
rope
rough
round
run

S
safe
sail
saw
scale
school
score
scrape
scratch
screen
seal
season
send
senior
service
set
settle
shade
shaft
shape
sharp
sheet
ship
shock
short
shoulder
show
shower
side
sign
sink
sit

skate
skin
skip
slide
slip
slow
slug
smart
smooth
snap
soil
sole
solid
space
spell
spin
spot
spread
spring
square
squash
squeeze
stab
stage
stake
stalk
stamp
stand
staple
state
station
steady
stem
stick
still
stir
stock
stone
string
strip
stroke
suit
sweep

T
table
tackle
tag
take
tap
tape

taste
tear
temple
tend
thread
tie
tight
time
title
touch
trace
track
trade
trail
train
trip
turn

U
unit
upset
use

V
vision
voice

W
walk
watch
wave
wax
way
wear
web
well
will
wind
word
work
wound

Power Idioms and Idiomatic Expressions

Idiom	Meaning
a bit much	excessive
a day late	too little too late
a hard place	alternatives
a lick and a promise	do something in a hurry
a long row to hoe	task that takes a long time
a penny for your thoughts	ask someone their thoughts
a pretty penny	cost a lot
a steal	cheap
about face	change your mind
above board	doing something legally
absent-minded	to be forgetful
across the board	applies to everyone
add fuel to the fire	make a bad situation worse
add insult to injury	make a situation worse
afraid of one's own shadow	frightened
against the grain	go against your beliefs
all ears	you want to hear all about something
all of a sudden	suddenly
all set	ready to begin
all your eggs in one basket	you risk everything
angry as a bear	very angry, furious
apple pie order	perfect order
arm in arm	linked arms

around the clock	open 24 hours
as a last resort	if everything else fails
as a rule	usually
as far as possible	do what you can
as the crow flies	the shortest distance
asleep at the wheel	not thinking
at a loss	can't understand
at arm's length	safe distance away
at loose ends	you don't know what to do
at wit's end	don't know what to do
AWOL	absent without leave
axe to grind	you have some resentment
back to back	one after another
back to square one	start at the beginning
backseat driver	giving advice to the driver
baker's dozen	13 instead of 12
ballpark figure	approximate number
be out in left field	not know what's going on
between a rock and a hard place	you are between two bad alternatives
between you me and the and the cat's whiskers	It's a secret
bird's eye view	see something very clearly
bite the bullet	do what you don't want to do
blind as a bat	in total darkness
bottom line	net income
bread winner	the person who earns the money
bring on board	bring someone on the team

burst at the seams	to be filled beyond capacity
by heart	memorize word for word
by leaps and bounds	something that happens quickly
by the skin of your teeth	you just managed to do something
by word of mouth	someone tells you about something
dead right	someone who is absolutely correct
deep pockets	someone who is very wealthy
dig in your heels	you resist doing something
don't cry over spilt milk	don't cry over something done in the past
drop someone a line	send a letter or email to someone
earn a living	work
easy as ABC	something is very easy
give up the ghost	die
hit and miss	unpredictable
like clockwork	something goes very well
like pulling teeth	something is very difficult
living on a shoestring	not much money
raining cats and dogs	raining very hard
safe and sound	safe
safe bet	seems certain
saved by the bell	saved just in time
take your hat off	showing respect
tit for tat	you get back at someone
under your breath	say something quietly
without a hitch	something goes well without a problem

Word Origins: States in the United States

Word	Origin
Alabama	named after the "Alibamu" Nation
Alaska	"Aleut" or great land
Arkansas	from the Quapaw Nation
California	from a book Las Sergias de Esplandian
Colorado	from Spanish "red"
Connecticut	Quinnehtukqut or "beside the long river"
Delaware	named after Sir Thomas West
Florida	from Spanish "feast of flowers"
Georgia	in honor of George II of England
Hawaii	named by the Polynesians
Indiana	land of the Indians
Maryland	named in honor of Henrietta Maria
Massachusetts	from Algonquinn "The people who live near the great hill", refers to Massachusett nation
Michigan	from the Indian word "Michigama" meaning large lake in Chippewa
Montana	from the Spanish word for mountain
Nebraska	from the Otto Indian meaning "flat water"
New Hampshire	from the English county of Hampshire

Interdisciplinary Vocabulary Development: The Rule of 3

English Language Arts Content Standards: Vocabulary and Concept Development

Kindergarten

- Identify and sort common words from basic categories (e.g., colors, shapes and foods).

- Describe common objects and events in both general and specific language.

First Grade

- Classify grade-appropriate categories of words (e.g., concrete collections of animals, food, toys).

Second Grade

- Understand and explain common antonyms and synonyms.

- Use knowledge of individual words in unknown compound words to predict their meaning.

- Know the meaning of simple prefixes and suffixes (e.g., *over-, un-, -ing, -ly*).

- Identify simple multiple-meaning words.

Third Grade

- Use knowledge of antonyms, synonyms, homophones and homographs to determine the meanings of words.

- Demonstrate knowledge of levels of specificity among grade-appropriate words, and explain the importance of these relations (e.g., dog/mammal/animal/living things).

- Use sentence and word context to find the meaning of unknown words.

- Use a dictionary to learn the meaning and other features of unknown words.

- Use knowledge of prefixes (e.g., *un-, re-, pre-, bi-, mis-, dis-*) and suffixes (e.g., *-er, -est, -ful*) to determine the meaning of words.

Fourth Grade

- Apply knowledge of word origins, derivations, synonyms, antonyms and idioms to determine the meaning of words and phrases.

- Use knowledge of root words to determine the meaning of unknown words within a passage.

- Know common roots and affixes derived from Greek and Latin and use this knowledge to analyze the meaning of complex words (e.g., international).

- Use a thesaurus to determine related words and concepts.

- Distinguish between and interpret words with multiple meanings.

Fifth Grade

- Use word origins to determine the meaning of unknown words.

- Understand and explain frequently used synonyms, antonyms and homographs.

- Know abstract, derived roots and affixes from Greek and Latin and use this knowledge to analyze the meaning of complex words (e.g., controversial).

- Understand and explain the figurative and metaphorical use of words in context.

Sixth Grade

- Identify and interpret figurative language and words with multiple meanings.

- Recognize the origins and meanings of frequently used foreign words in English and use these words accurately in speaking and writing.

- Monitor expository text for unknown words or words with novel meanings by using word, sentence and paragraph clues to determine meaning.

- Understand and explain "shades of meaning" in related words (e.g., softly and quietly).

Seventh Grade

- Identify idioms, analogies, metaphors and similes in prose and poetry.

- Use knowledge of Greek, Latin and Anglo-Saxon roots and affixes to understand content-area vocabulary.

- Clarify word meanings through the use of definitions, example, restatement or contrast.

Eighth Grade

- Analyze idioms, analogies, metaphors and similes to infer the literal and figurative meaning of phrases.

- Understand the most important points in the history of the English language and use common word origins.

- Use word meanings within the appropriate context and show ability to verify those meanings by definition, restatement, example, comparison or contrast.

Ninth and Tenth Grades

- Identify and use the literal and figurative meaning of words.

- Distinguish between the denotative and connotative meanings of words.

- Identify Greek, Roman and Norse mythology and use the knowledge to understand the origin and meaning of new words.

Eleventh and Twelfth Grades

- Trace the etymology of significant terms used in political science and history.

- Apply knowledge of Greek, Latin and Anglo-Saxon roots and affixes to draw inferences.

- Discern the meaning of analogies analyzing specific comparisons as well as relationships and inferences.

Bibliography

Aglioti, S. (1996). Neurolinguistic Follow-Up Study. *Brain*, 119.

Anderson, J.R. and Reder, L.M. (2002). An elaborate processing explanation of depth of processing. In L.S. Cermack and F.M. Craik (Eds.), *Levels of processing in human memory*. Hillsdale: Erlbaum Associates.

Anderson, R.C., and Nagy, W.E. (1991). Word meanings. In R. Barr, M.L. Kamil, P.B. Mosenthal, & P.D. Pearson (Eds.), *Handbook of reading research*. (951-982). New York: Longman.

Armbruster, BB & Nagy, W.E. (1992). Research on vocabulary instruction in the content areas: Implications for struggling readers. In J. Flood, J.M. Jenson, D. Lapp, and J.R. Squire (Eds.), *Handbook on teaching the English language arts*, 602–632.

August, D., Calderon, M., and Carlo, M. (2002). *Transfer of reading skills from Spanish to English: A study of young learners*. Report ED-98-CO-0071.

Baker, C. (1993). Foundations *of bilingual education and bilingualism*. Philadelphia: Multilingual Matters.

Baldwin, R. and Schutz, E. (1986). Context clues are ineffective with low frequency words in naturally occurring prose. In J.A. Niles and L. A. Harris (Eds.), *New inquiries in research and instruction 31st yearbook*. Newark, DE: National Reading Association.

Barr, R., Kamil, M.L., Mosenthal,P.B., and Peasrson, P.D. (Eds.). (1991). *Handbook of reading research*. New York: Longman.

Barron, R.F. (1999). The use of vocabulary as an advance organizer. In H.L. Herber and P.L. Sanders (Eds.), First year report. Syracuse: New York: Syracuse University Press.

Baumann, J.F. and Kameerun. (1991). Research on vocabulary: Ode to Voltaire. In J. Flood, J. Jensen, D. Lapp and J. Squire (Eds.), *Handbook of research on teaching English language arts* (pp. 601-632). New York: Macmillan.

Bear, D. Invernizzi, M., Templeton, S. and Johnston, F. (1991). Words their way: Word study of phonics, vocabulary and spelling instruction. In R. Barr, M. Kamil, P. Mosenthal and P.D. Pearson (Eds.), *Handbook on reading research*. New York: Longman.

Beck, L. and McCaslin, E.S. (1978). An analysis of dimensions that affect the development of code breaking ability in eight beginning reading programs. *LRDC Report No. 1978/6*. Pittsburgh: University of Pittsburgh Research and Development Center.

Beck, I.L. and McKeown, M.G. and Kucan, L. (2002). *Bringing words to life: Robust vocabulary*. NewYork: Guilford.

Beck, I. L. and McKeown, M. (1991). Conditions of vocabulary acquisition. In R. Barr, M. Kamil, P. Mosenthal and P.D. Pearson (Eds.), *Handbook on reading research (506-521)*. New York: Longman.

Beck, I. L., Perfetti, C.A. and Mckeown, M.G. (1982). Effects of long term vocabulary instruction on lexical access and reading comprehension. *Journal of Educational Psychology, 74*, 506-521.

Beck, I.L., McKeown, M.G. and Omanson, R.C. (2002). The effects and uses of diverse vocabulary instructional techniques. In M.C. Mckeown and M.E. Curtis (Eds.), *The nature of vocabulary acquisition*. Hillsdale: Erlbaum Associates.

Blachowicz, C. and Fisher, P. (2000). Teaching vocabulary. In R. Barr, M. Kamil, P. Mosenthal and P.D. Pearson (Eds.), *Handbook on reading research (503-523)*. New York: Longman.

Blachowicz, C. (1987). Vocabulary instruction: What goes on in the classroom? *Reading Teacher, 41*, 130-137.

Blanton, W. and Morrman, G. (1990). The presentation of reading lessons. *Reading Research and Instruction, 29, 31*, 33-55.

Braham, C., Pearsons, E. Sheildlower, J. and Cook, C. (Eds.), (1990). *Random House Webster's build your personal vocabulary*. New York: Random House.

Cummins, J. (2000). *Language power and pedagogy: Bilingual children in the crossfire.* Clevedon, England: Multilingual Matters.

Calderon, M. (2004). *Study on transition: Evidence base for practice.* Center for Data Driven Reform in Education.

California State Board of Education. (2004). *Science framework for California public schools.* Sacramento: California.

California State Board of Education. (2000). *Reading language arts framework for California public schools.* Sacramento: California.

California State Board of Education. (2002). *English language development standards for California public schools.* Sacramento: California.

Carlo, M., August D., McLaughlin, B., Snow, C. et al. *Closing the Gap: Addressing the Vocabulary Needs of English Language Learners in Bilingual and Mainstream Classrooms.* Reading Research Quarterly, 39 (2) (2004): 188-189, 1991-218.

Cassie, K. Vocabulary Building for the Intermediate Student. A TESOL Professional Anthology, The Primary and Elementary Classroom, edited by Carol Cargill. Lincolnwood: National Textbook, (1990).

Dole, J., Sloan, C. and Trathen, W. (1995). Teaching vocabulary within the context of literature. *Journal of Reading*, 38, 452, 460.

Dunn, M., Bonner, B. and Huske, L. (2007). *Developing a systems process for improving instruction in vocabulary: Lessons learned.* Alexandria, Virginia: Association of Supervision and Curriculum Development.

Durkin, D. (1966). *Children who read early: Two longitudinal studies.* New York: Teachers College Press.

Durkin, D. (1979). What classroom observations reveal about reading comprehension instruction. *Reading Research Quarterly*, 14, 481-533.

Fillmore, L.W. and Snow, C. (2000) What teachers need to know about language. *ERIC Special Report.* Washington D.C.: Center for Applied Linguistics.

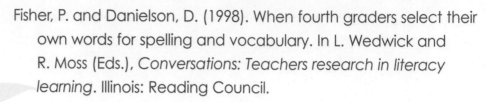

Fisher, P. and Danielson, D. (1998). When fourth graders select their own words for spelling and vocabulary. In L. Wedwick and R. Moss (Eds.), *Conversations: Teachers research in literacy learning*. Illinois: Reading Council.

Flynt, S. and Brozo, W. (2008). Developing Academic Language: Got Words. *The Reading Teacher*, 6, 16.

Frid, L. (2008). *The integration of sciences*. Unpublished manuscript.

Gottlieb, H. (2003). Language political implications of subtitling. In P. Obereo, *Topics in audiovisual translation*. Leeds, U.K.: Centre for Translations Studies.

Graves, M.F. (2000). A vocabulary program to complement and bolster a middle-grade comprehension program. In B.M. Taylor, M.F. Graves and P. van den Broek (Eds.), *Reading for meaning: Fostering comprehension in the middle grades*. New York: Teachers College Press.

Graves, M.F. (1986). Vocabulary learning and instruction. In E.Z. Rothkopt and L.C. Ehri (Eds.), *Review of research in education*. Washington D.C.: American Educational Research Association.

Graves. M.F., Watts, S. and Taffe, S. (2002). Disadvantaged students are likely to have substantially smaller vocabularies than their more advantaged classmates. In A. Farstrup and S.J. Samuels (Eds.). *What research has to say about reading instruction*. Newark, DE: International Reading Association.

Graves. M.F., Watts, S. and Taffe, S. (2002). The place of word consciousness in a research-based vocabulary program. In A. Farstrup and S.J. Samuels (Eds.), *What research has to say about reading instruction*. Newark, DE: International Reading Association.

Gulatt, D.E. (1987). How to help students in reading mathematics. *The Education Digest*, 52,5,40.

Haggard, M.R. (1982). The vocabulary self selection strategy: An active approach to word learning. *Journal of Reading*, 29, 634-642.

Harmon, J.M., Hedrick, W.B, and Fox, E.A. (2000). A content analysis of vocabulary instruction in social studies textbooks for grades 4-8. *The Elementary School Journal,* 190, 3, 253-271.

Harmon, J.M., Hedrick, W.B. and Wood, K.D. (2005). Research on vocabulary instruction in the content areas: Implications for struggling readers. *Reading and Writing Quarterly,* 21, 261-280.

Heath, S.B. (1983). *Ways with words.* Cambridge: Cambridge University Press.

Hiebert, E. and Kamil, M. (2005). *Teaching and learning vocabulary: Bringing research to practice.* New York: Routledge.

Jaeger-Adams, M. (1996). *Beginning to read.* Cambridge, Massachusetts: MIT Press.

Jenkins, Joseph R.; Dixon, Robert. (1983). Vocabulary learning. *Educational Psychology,* 8, 3, 237-60.

Juel, C. (1983). The development and use of mediated word identification. *Reading Research Quarterly,* 18, 306-327.

Juel, C., Roper/Schneider, D. (1985). The influence of basal readers on first grade reading. *Reading Research Quarterly,* 20, 134-152.

Kameenui, E.J., Carnine, D.W. and Freschi, R. (1982). The effects of text construction and instructional procedures for teaching word meanings on comprehension and recall. *Reading Research Quarterly,* 17, 367-388.

Kamil, M.L. (2004). Vocabulary and comprehension instruction: Summary and implications of the National Reading Panel findings. In P. McCardle and V. Cnhabra (Eds.), *The voice of evidence in reading research.* Baltimore, Maryland: Paul H. Brookes.

Klein, D. (2008).Unsupervised learning for natural language processing. *Colt,* 5-6.

Laflamme, J. G. (1997). The effect of multiple exposures to vocabulary methods and the target reading and writing strategy on test scores. *Journal of Adolescent and Adult Literacy, 40*, 5, 372-384.

Marshall, S. and Gillmore, M. (1991). Words that matter in science and technology: A study of Papua New Guinean students comprehension of non technical words used in science and technology. *Research in Science and Technological Education, 9*, 1. 5-16.

Marzano, R. (2004). *Building background knowledge for academic achievement: Research on what works in schools.* Alexandria, Virginia: Association of Supervision and Curriculum Development.

Marzano, R. (2005). *Preliminary report on the 2004-2005 evaluation of the ACSD program for building academic vocabulary.* Alexandria, Virginia: Association of Supervision and Curriculum Development.

McGinley, W.J. and Denner, P.R. (1987) Story Impressions: A prereading writing activity. *Journal of Reading, 31*, 248-254.

McKeown, M. (1993). *Creating word definitions for young word learners.* Reading Research Quarterly, 28, 16-33.

McKeown, M. (1991). Learning word meanings from definitions: Problems and potential. In P. Schwanedflugel (Ed.), *The psychology of word meanings.* Hillsdale: Erlbaum.

McKeown, M., Beck, I., Omanson, R.C. and Perfetti, C.A. (1983). The effects of long term vocabulary instruction on reading comprehension: A replication. *Journal of Reading Behavior, 15*, 3-18.

McKeown, M., Beck, I., Omanson, R.C. and Pople, M.T. Some effects of the nature and frequency of vocabulary instruction on the knowledge and use of words. *Reading Research Quarterly, 20*, 522-535, 1985.

Meyer, P., Jezzard, M., Adams, M. and Turner, R. (1995). *Functional evidence for adult motor plasticity during motor skill.* National Institute of Health Report.

Monroe, E.E. (1997). Effects of mathematical instruction on fourth grade students. *Reading Improvement,* 34, 120-132.

Monroe, E.E. and Panchyahyn, R. (1995). Vocabulary considerations for teaching mathematics. *Childhood Education, 72,2,* 80-83.

Myers, K. (1996). Twenty better questions. *Journal of Adolescent and Adult Literacy,* 39, 5.

Nagy, W.E. (1997). On the role of context in first and second language vocabulary learning. In N. Schmitt and McCarthy L. (Eds.), *Vocabulary: Description, acquisition and pedagogy.* Cambridge: Cambridge University Press.

Nagy, W. E. (1988). *Teaching vocabulary to improve reading comprehension.* Newark, DE: International Reading Association.

Nagy, W.E. and Anderson, R.C. (1984). How many words are there in printed school English? *Reading Research Quarterly.* 19, 304-330.

Nagy, W.E. and Herman, P.A. (1997). Breadth and depth of vocabulary knowledge: Implications for acquisition and instruction. In McKeown, M.G. and Curtis, M. *The nature of vocabulary acquisition.* Hillsdale, New Jersey: Erlbaum Associates.

Nagy, W.E. and Scott J. (2000). Vocabulary processing. In M. Kamil, P., P.D. Pearson and R. Barr (Eds.), *Handbook of reading research.* New Jersey: Erlbaum.

Nagy, W.E. and Scott, J.A. (2000). Vocabulary processes. In M.L. Kamil, P. Mosenthal, P.D. Pearson, & R. Barr (Eds.), *Handbook of reading research.* New York: Longman.

Nation, I.S.P. (2001). *Learning vocabulary in another language.* Cambridge, England: Cambridge University Press.

Nelson, G.L. and Carlson, J.G. (1996). ESL students perceptions of effectiveness in peer response groups. *Journal of Second Language Writing,* 7, 113,131.

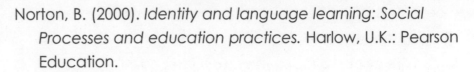

Norton, B. (2000). *Identity and language learning: Social Processes and education practices.* Harlow, U.K.: Pearson Education.

Paribakht, T.S. and Welshe, M. (1996). Enhancing vocabulary acquisition through reading: A hierarchy of text-related exercise types. *Canadian Modern Language Review, 5,* 155-176.

Rand Reading Study Group. (2003). *Reading for Understanding: Toward an R&D program in reading comprehension.* Santa Monica: Rand.

Ruff, T.P. and Milligan, J. L.(1990). A linguistic approach to social studies vocabulary development. *The Social Studies, 81,* 218–220.

Scartella, R. and Rumberger, R.W. (2000). *Academic English: A conceptual framework.* Riverside: University of California Linguistic Minority Research Institute.

Schwartz, R. and Raphael, T. (1985). Concept of definition: A key to improving students' vocabulary. *Reading Teacher, 39,* 198-205.

Scott, J., Jamieson, Noel and Asselin, Marlene. (2003). Vocabulary instruction throughout the day in twenty-three Canadian upper elementary classrooms. *Elementary School Journal, 103,* 7.

Simpson, J. (2007). Review of the struggle to teach English as an international language. *Applied Linguistics, 28,1, 147-150.*

Stahl, S.A. and Fairbanks, M. (1986). The effects of vocabulary instruction: A model-based meta-analysis. *Review of Education Research, 56, 1, 72-110.*

Stotsky, S. (1983). Research on reading/writing relationships: A syntheses and suggested directions. *Language Arts, 60,* 627-742.

Svetlana, Nikita. (2003). Three strategies for interdisciplinary science teaching. *Project Zero Report:* Harvard Graduate School.

Thomas, Wayne and Collier, Virginia. (2002). A national study of school effectiveness for language minority students' long term academic achievement. *Final report: Executive summary*. Center for Research on Education and Diversity.

Venet, B. (2008). *Mathematical poetry*. San Diego, California. Unpublished.

Ventriglia, Linda. (1992). *Conversations of Miguel and Maria: How children learn a second language*. New York: Pearson.

Ventriglia, Linda. (2008). *Best practices in vocabulary development: The rule of 3*. Sacramento: YounglightEducate.

Wade, Henry. (2008). The language readers: Primer. *BiblioBazaar: LLC*.

Walsh, K. (2003). Basal Readers: The lost opportunity to build knowledge that propels comprehension. *American Educator*, 27, 24-27.

Watts, S. (1995). Vocabulary instruction during reading lessons in six classrooms. *Journal of Reading Behavior*, 27, 399-424.

Weizman, Z. and Snow, C. (2004). Lexical input as related to children's vocabulary acquisition: Effects of sophisticated exposure and support for meaning. *Developmental Psychology*, 37, 265-279.

Wells, G. (1985). Preschool literacy-related activities and success in school. In D. Olson, N. Torrance and A. Hildyard (Eds.), *Literacy, language and learning: The nature and consequences of reading and writing*. New York: Cambridge University Press.

Zadina, J. (2005). *Brain research and second language learners*. English learner keynote speech. Washington D.C.: United States Department of Education.

Zentella, A.C. (1997). *Growing up bilingual*. Massachusetts: Blackwell.

About the Author

Linda Ventriglia is the Director of the Center for Teaching Excellence. She has a Ph.D. in Curriculum and Instruction and a Masters in Public Administration from Claremont University and Harvard University. She also completed three years postdoctoral research at Harvard in second language acquisition and literacy development. A former teacher and school psychologist, Dr. Ventriglia has served as an educational consultant across the United States and internationally. She has also served as Chief Consultant to the California State Legislature on the Education and Workforce subcommittee. Dr. Ventriglia is the author of *Conversations of Miguel and Maria: How Children Learn a Second Language (Pearson)*, *Ready for English* (National Textbook), *Santillana Intensive English* (Santillana U.S.A.), *Teaching Strategies for the 21st Century*, and the *Best Practices in Education series*. Dr. Ventriglia has received a number of grants and has done national and international research on effective learning strategies. Dr. Ventriglia has also written a number of articles and has been featured in educational journals including the *California Educator*.